the
SISTERHOOD
of WIDOWS

Sixteen True Stories *of*
Grief, Anger *and* Healing

MARY FRANCIS

Morgan James Publishing • NEW YORK

the SISTERHOOD of WIDOWS

ISBN: 978-1-60037-779-2 (Paperback)
Library of Congress Control Number: 2010922578

Published by:
MORGAN JAMES PUBLISHING
1225 Franklin Ave Ste 32
Garden City, NY 11530-1693
Toll Free 800-485-4943
www.MorganJamesPublishing.com

Cover/Interior Design by:
Rachel Lopez
rachel@r2cdesign.com

In an effort to support local communities, raise awareness and funds, Morgan James Publishing donates one percent of all book sales for the life of each book to Habitat for Humanity. Get involved today, visit **www.HelpHabitatForHumanity.org.**

Dedication

This book is dedicated to my beloved husband, Donnie.
Thank you for the twenty-seven year chapter in my life's book.

And

To all the widows, young and old, who
are weathering the tailspin of that first year.

Testimonials

Mary Francis has mapped a journey that none of us wish to embark upon; widowhood. This book chronicles the experiences of sixteen women who have made that journey revealing the host of emotions and challenges they encountered along the way. If you've been widowed your journey will be unique, but I believe you will find comfort, strength and inspiration in the courage that is the common thread here. In the equally brave act of sharing their stories, these women have offered a gift to those who will follow in these difficult footsteps.

—HOLLY REID
*Preplanner/Aftercare Advisor,
Brenan's Funeral Homes, Saint John,
New Brunswick, Canada*

Finally! A motivational book to help widow's face an incredibly difficult time. The life lessons they share reveal their raw and real experiences—

emotionally, financially and physically. In the health care profession, we see women put themselves last in a crisis and their health deteriorates because of it. This book is a wonderful collection of "life after loss" experiences and how women not only survive, but find a way to thrive.

—NATALIE TREADWELL
Founder of Food For Life Healthy Lifestyle

Having my mother widowed at a young age, I experienced first hand the trials and tribulations she faced being left with four young children. As an adult, reading these pages has helped me to relate to how and why my mother dug in to overcome the daunting emotional and financial obstacles she faced. Being a strong mother and father figure she instilled strong spirituality, morality and work ethics into her children, making all of us what we are today.

A book of this nature would have been a tremendous support to her at that time, just knowing she wasn't alone. I am very confident that this collection of intimate stories will not only help, but will put widows in a place of hope which they may never have thought possible.

—STEPHEN SPIRES, *Owner, Smet Monuments*

The majority of society chooses not to speak of death and loss. As a Hospice Patient-Family Volunteer I have been with loved ones that will not seek help that choose to carry on and never get past their feelings of guilt and loss. Those feelings affect their lives and those they love on many levels and will prevent them from having an abundant life.

Mary Francis has provided a light through the tunnel of grief and a source of comfort and understanding to widows that only someone who has endured this kind of loss can provide.

—DEBORAH RYAN
Hospice Patient-Family Volunteer

I applaud Mary's ability to both recognize a definite need for widows who are coping with the loss of their husband, and her fortitude and approach in completing this work. Mary, as a recent widow, was able to realize that only a widow can offer the best advice to another widow. Each testimony gives different insight and understanding into the transition of wife to widow. These testimonies layered together under one cover, offer a needed comfort to a new widow.

Mary gives the reader the opportunity to write their own chapter and formulate their own healing strategy by translating the personal testimonies of fifteen widows and adding her own. Well done.

—TODD D SOPER
President, Todd D Soper Financial Services Inc.

In reading the short stories about widows by Mary Francis she has brought out the true meaning of "Sisterhood". Many women of today do not realize their strengths of durability, tenacity and most of all resilience. She is letting the world know the true strength of our gender.

I am associated with a very fun "Sisterhood" known as "The Red Hat Society" where I have the privilege of witnessing acts of "Sisterhood" constantly.

—DIANNE O'BRIEN
[Red Hat Queen of The Lucky Lady Bugs]

Mary has provided us with a collection of stories that are both moving and inspiring. I recommend this book to those who grieve, who need to know they are not alone in how they feel and think. I also recommend it to Pastors, like myself, who need to be reminded of what it is like to walk through the valley of the shadow of death.

—PASTOR EDWARD POWELL
Grand Bay Baptist Church

Some of us can only imagine the many emotions experienced by Mary Francis and the widows who contributed to this amazing book. Each woman's story is unique yet similar in many ways. Though their pain, anger, fear and loneliness are at times overwhelming to read, always present in the fabric of their stories is a sense of hope and in many cases a strong faith.

Embodied in each of these women is the strength that it takes to overcome adversity and without question they teach us all the meaning of resilience and survival and they do so in their own words. No doubt Mary has provided an opportunity for these women to experience healing as they shared their stories and now that same healing can be felt by countless others as they read "The Sisterhood of Widows."

—**TRACY FRIARS**
*Lay Worship Leader
and Human Resource Consultant*

Acknowledgements

When I became a widow I went looking for information, but found my healing in the stories of other widows. They helped me to understand that it's normal to be unbalanced and emotional when your husband dies. Their names have been changed in the book, but they know who they are and I want to thank them for sharing their stories. They were truthful about all the emotions they felt: the good, the bad and the ugly. When you read their stories, may it give you comfort to know that others have traveled your path and understand your grief. From the deepest part of my heart I would like to thank all the widows who found within themselves the strength to share their difficulties and their triumphs with me.

I couldn't have done this book without the constant support and love of my family and friends. I cherish my sisters, Nancy, Jane, Joyce and Joy for believing in me. Also, thanks to my sisterhood at work (Kathy, Lynn, Cynthia, Mary Jane, Norma and yes Chris) for supporting and listening to me while I worked on the book.

I appreciate Holly Reid, at Brenan's Funeral Home, for her encouragement and support. When I first expressed the idea of the book for new widows, Holly understood why I was drawn to do it. Todd Soper, at Sun Life Financial supported my vision and offered his encouragement. Todd believed in the early, rough draft of the manuscript and had the vision to see this book.

Thanks to Glenn and Deb Lankin for their proof reading of the book and to Pat Perrin for reading rough drafts, offering constructive criticism and doing a poem for the book. I think Cindy Kohler did an outstanding job on the book cover. She really understood my vision for the cover and was able to capture it.

I also wish to acknowledge the editing skill and wise counsel of Jill Eckstone. Jill deserves special mention for she contributed greatly to the organization of this book and made it possible to submit it to the publisher with a finished look.

I found an evening out at Carleton Curling Club for the Business Ladies League. They were open to a new member that was kind of lost and sad. They are a great group of ladies who define what a sisterhood is all about. Another fantastic group of ladies are my "Red Hat" sisters (www.redhatsociety.com) because they have shown me how to laugh and be silly. Truly nothing helps you heal better then getting out and enjoying your friends and family.

To my children, Nathan and Angela, for being there for me these last few years. I love you both and I'm very proud of you. A special thanks to my daughter in-law, Andrea, for taking such good care of Nathan. It gives me peace of mind to know you have each other.

Foreword

My husband died at the age of fifty-three and so I became a widow at the age of fifty. Twenty-seven years of marriage and now I'm single, but I don't feel like I'm single. In fact I'm not married, not divorced and really not single—and so I'm a Widow. How odd that seems!

I didn't want to go to group meetings or see a counselor (it just wasn't for me) so I turned to other widows to find my answers. We were different widows, just like we were different wives, and I found parts of myself in the experiences that the other widows had before me.

It never occurred to me during the years I was putting my life together—family, business, home, and finances—that one day I would have to start all over. Suddenly, I have been given a wide array of new choices—in effect, a second life. I asked myself—Where do I start?

There's a lot going on in this world and you're not going to know about it unless you get out. Let's be realistic—you can't go after what you want if you don't know what's available. Depression and anger can be overwhelming after the death of your husband. Resilience is being able to stand up to the uncertainty, the unknown and to become a stronger woman as a result.

Don't waste your time thinking it's too late to go after your dreams. You can learn new things at any time in your life if you're willing to be a beginner. When it comes to dreams—nobody makes you do them. Nobody is going to push you. You have to do it for yourself.

Although not for everyone, professional help can be just what you need to understand that it's normal to be so unbalanced. If you want to talk to someone that can help you with the emotions that you're faced with, then get a counselor that you're comfortable with. Ask other widows if they know of anyone that can help you, look up the local community health clinic or ask your family doctor for a referral. Don't hold back, this is the time to reach out.

The sisterhood of widows isn't a blood tie, but women bond together in a special way that makes us like a family. We share the parts of our lives that only other women can understand. It is important to spend time with a family of women to nurture and support ourselves. To be listened to, humored and encouraged by our women friends is a gift not to be taken lightly. The book "The Sisterhood of Widows" was born from the idea that we are all sisters in the emotions we carry and that there should be one book that tells it all.

The book is passionate and at times the anger leaps off the pages. It is truthful and sometimes painful. Perhaps that's why it is such a powerful book of healing. As I find myself walking on this unknown path I know that others have gone before me. That is somehow reassuring to me. So reach out to other widows, they understand like no one else can.

Table of Contents

I used the iris symbol throughout the book because the primary meaning of the word "iris" includes faith, hope, wisdom, courage and admiration.

It also means the rainbow or *courage after a difficult time*.

www.thesisterhoodofwidows.com

Chapter 1

TAKE THE TIME TO REALLY LEARN WHO YOU ARE

By continually facing your problems honestly and objectively,
you become a more confident and competent person.
You become stronger and more self-reliant.

—BRIAN TRACY, *Maximum Achievement*

I had lost a pregnancy and thought it would be hard for me to get pregnant again. Adoption was a long wait unless we would consider a non-white child, so when the opportunity came to adopt James, at eight months of age, we simply took it. Little did we know what was about to happen. A few months after adopting our baby boy, I scheduled a doctor's appointment for what I thought was a bladder infection.

"I have the flu and maybe a bladder infection. I'm getting up in the middle of the night to pee." The doctor started laughing and asked if it had occurred to me that I might be pregnant. That's how we got started. Our three boys were within three years of each other. James appeared to be the catalyst to the next two boys and our family of three was now five.

James was just this great kid until his fifteenth year when drugs took control of his life. I don't know whether the fact that he was adopted or that he was half black in a white family was what drove him into this dark period of his life.

As parents, both of us dealt with what James was doing much differently. Mike, a Police Officer, believed in strict discipline. He wouldn't meet James half way; give up the drugs, period. I, on the other hand, reacted by crying and begging Mike to work with him, but they would always end up fighting. Several times James was told to leave. He would eventually come back home, but the effect on the two younger boys was not good.

James was living in the south end of the city and was in constant trouble. He decided to move across the country, and we were relieved because with all of the torment and troubles, we just wanted him out of our lives. It was too much stress on our marriage and on the other two boys. James' name had been in the paper and Mike was extremely ashamed. You couldn't buy James a job because he had such a bad reputation. James would call once in a while for money or to talk and even once to tell us that he had gone to a rehab center. He sent us a wonderful letter but when he got out, he went back into his old life and once again drugs controlled him. Mike still had contacts with the police force and a friend would check the system to see if James was in or out of jail.

James was out of our lives, but the guilt we lived with was unbearable. We never went to visit him and kept hoping he would get well and come back home with his act together. But that was not in the cards and James ended up committing suicide.

The last six years of his life he lived alone and I didn't want him to come home, because I didn't think my nerves could take it. Mike couldn't take it either and our marriage suffered greatly, but how can you turn your back on your child and live with it? I can't even begin to tell you the guilt I felt.

James was one tough little customer and I never would have thought that he would consider suicide. I am not sure what he was thinking, but he must have felt that he couldn't pull himself up again and just gave up. Losing our son, James, is something I will never get over and there are really no words to express how I feel. Your children just shouldn't die before you.

At one point James had a really nice girlfriend that we used to talk on the phone with. I spoke with her when they broke up.

She said, "I just can't take it anymore. He has sold my TV and this and that."

James would get frantic for drugs and would do anything for the money to buy them. As a youngster, he would sell all the stuff we bought him for drug money. Mike and I never really talked about it and so it became another unresolved issue in my life. I wish we had gone to visit James before he died. There are still so many things I don't have closure to and now I never will. James died alone and must have felt we never loved him. How can I live with that? I went to a counselor because I was tormented that I had not made an effort to go see James when he was alive.

I was always a good girl, but if I did foolish things I knew it was my decision and not the fault of my parents. I have so much guilt over the death of my son that sometimes it just chokes me. Mike's parenting policy of tough love and my much gentler approach caused many arguments.

Counseling didn't help repair the rift that was growing between us during James' life nor repair the damage that was done when his life was over.

When Mike started drinking again after eight years, I was very angry. Whenever he got upset he would escape to the Legion and leave me at home alone to deal with whatever was making him mad. I couldn't always count on him when I needed him the most.

I felt that he was nothing more than a hypocrite when he talked about James' drug habit. Our family of five, once surrounded with joy and full of life, was suddenly immersed in darkness and anger.

It was about six months after James died that we moved out to the country. Despite all the troubles with James, I have a lot of good memories of our old home. Memories of the kid's tree house, the pool table, the basketball games and the wonderful family times still remain with me today. This new house in the country helped Mike and I grow closer, but the core of me still blamed him for the troubles we had in our family. Little did I know there were more troubles on the way.

Mike was losing weight and seemed tired a lot. His stomach bothered him and at one point I thought he had gallstones. We thought they would have to remove his gall bladder, but he golfed every day and seemed healthy so I really wasn't all that concerned. By the time they diagnosed him with pancreatic cancer it was too late. There are no words to describe the impact of that single word: CANCER.

When my father died ten years ago, they said they couldn't treat the cancer, but they could treat the man because they knew he wouldn't live long enough to receive chemotherapy treatments. I remember telling him that they just wanted to build him up for it.

I couldn't bear to tell him the truth because Dad was in his seventies and he wanted to live longer. But when Mike first got sick they were going to put him on chemo and that gave me hope that he was going to be OK.

Later Mike was very sick, but they released him from the hospital. I suppose there wasn't anything they could do for him there than I couldn't do for him at home. I asked the nurse when I should bring him back. She just looked at me and said, "you will know." I had no idea what she meant at the time, but she was right. When the time came I just knew.

Even though he was so sick we never talked about the cancer or what the future might hold. We avoided the subject. I'm sure Mike knew he was dying, but he didn't want to talk about it. What could either of us really say that would make any difference?

Mike didn't want to hear anything but positive thoughts that spoke about the future. I remember the Minister that came to visit Mike in the hospital. He didn't want her "talking gloom and doom" all the time. She would ask him if he was 'ready' and he didn't want to hear it. He did welcome Extra Mural; however, because they would talk about booking tests for him in a week's time and that gave him hope that he would recover.

We were married for thirty-five years when Mike died. We didn't preplan our funerals but I had an idea of what I wanted because of James funeral three years earlier. We had our cemetery plots because Mike's parents had bought them as part of the family plot. Paul, our second son, was thirty years old at the time of Mike's death. He took on such a leadership role in the preparations. We had Mike cremated and then held a memorial service at a local church. There was standing room only and I got Christmas poinsettias to place around his picture.

I think a lot of people saw the writing on the wall, but I was still in a daze. I wasn't anywhere near ready to accept that Mike was dead. The ladies in the church put on a luncheon and it couldn't have been better. Everyone was just so helpful and willing to do anything for me. The funeral parlor kept the ashes and in the spring we had a private burial service.

Mike had a lot of friends and he was involved in so many things that I just couldn't invite everyone to the burial. I was afraid that I wouldn't be able to keep it contained and too many people would be there so we kept it to a small service.

We had already put up our tombstone when James died and so all that was left was adding Mike's death date. Mike had everything organized so that it was easy for me when I went to the bank. It's hard to fill out all the forms and it all seems more difficult than it is because you just can't think. Even though everything was organized, there was still so much to do; different people to contact, death certificates to deal with and so much more.

I had to have $10,000.00 within thirty days to pay for everything when Mike died. It all went on my Visa until I got the paper work completed. I couldn't believe how expensive it was.

Thinking about it now, if I have any extra money I might look into prepaying my own funeral. I went in last fall to update my will and I also did a living will. After Mike's death, I realized how important it was to have your paper work done so your family doesn't have to deal with it.

Years ago Mike was on his way home from work when he came across a huge accident with lots of cars piled up on the highway. Mike got out of his car to help and was hit by a bus. He was hurt really bad and was never able to go back to work so he took an early pension.

Afterwards Mike went to university on student loans to get his degree. At that time he was on crutches and it was hard for him to get around. He had been admired for getting his degree with his leg all beat up. They had done over twenty-one operations on his leg. They really tried to save the leg, but in the end he lost it.

On the first anniversary of Mike's death we wanted to do something special in his memory. Paul went to the club his father had been a member of and arranged a golf tournament and dinner. It was a massive undertaking and over one hundred and fifty people attended. The auction raised a lot of money and all of it went to the university in Mike's name as a bursary to help students with disabilities get their degree. At the time, I wasn't really up for participating in the event but I knew that it would be a healing process for both the boys and I.

Time was moving on, but I was still locked in a sea of emotion ranging from guilt to grief to anger. Last summer I was visiting a friend and she knew I was having trouble coping. She knew this counselor and suggested I see him. I called him and we spoke for awhile on the phone. I told him about James dying and how I partly blamed my husband but then he died. I asked him to explain to me how I could be mad at a dead man.

I shared my feelings of grief and guilt and I told him I was angry and hurt. We talked about being stuck in the middle of two very different painful experiences and that I had to find a way to break through it all. I knew then I needed help and so I sought a counselor closer to where I lived. In time, she did help me to understand all the emotions I was going through.

All my friends would say, "You and Mike did everything you could do for James" but in my heart I didn't feel that we did. I had yet to realize that Mike did the best he knew how to do and I did everything I could. I had to learn to forgive Mike and myself.

Not an easy task and one that I am not sure I will ever truly achieve. Now I feel less anger, but I still have a lot of sadness and grief.

I said things to my counselor that I have never been able to say to anyone. There are some things that we just need to keep close to us. People knew James got into a lot of trouble, but I loved him because he was my son and people knew that there were issues with Mike, but I didn't want to tarnish his reputation or lead anyone to think anything bad about him.

The anger and hurt I was feeling after James and Mike died was eating me up inside. I had to find a way to rid myself of it. How could I be mad at Mike for dying? How sad that James was so hurt, so troubled inside that he felt he had no other choice but to take his own life?

I was terribly depressed after James died and then when Mike died three years later it almost sent me over the deep end. I was spending all my time in my bedroom watching TV. I wanted to do something, but I wasn't sure what. I didn't want to spend another Christmas feeling sad and off balanced.

I knew I had to pull myself together and that's when I decided to go to the Grand Cayman Islands. I had a place to stay for two weeks because my friend's daughter was coming home for Christmas. I didn't know when I would return and I didn't make any specific plans, so I purchased a one-way ticket and just went. I think I was willing to do just about anything to get out of my surroundings for awhile.

I did things that I never had an opportunity to do before, like swimming with the dolphins. I have a picture of me with the life jacket on and I just love it. I'm so proud of myself; renting a car and driving around the island, stretching myself and doing things I have never done before. I would go to the beach every day, read a book and go swimming. That was heaven to me and it allowed me that much needed time to begin healing.

When I was home, I felt like I was carrying around a two hundred pound bag of grief. I still carried the pain and grief in the Caymans, but I felt separated from it and in a way I felt lighter. It is almost impossible to explain and something that just simply existed; an entity unto itself. I felt relieved from the pressures of my life that I had been immersed in for so long a time.

I was so desperate after James and Mike died, for some sort of connection that I went to a psychic. I'm not sure if she was simply reading my emotions and then feeding them back to me, but she seemed sincere.

She picked up on the fact that James was a really troubled boy with a lot of demons and that his death was pretty well inevitable. A lot of stuff she did tell me was pretty amazing and when I went this past year she told me that I was going to go away. Perhaps she helped me to discover that I truly love living in the South. When I'm home I feel surrounded by sadness, but those feelings don't overwhelm me when I'm away in the Cayman Islands.

The high cost of going away is beginning to take its toll and I have to figure out a way of financing more visits. I thought about selling the house, but I have such great neighbors and they really look out for me. I have also thought about putting an apartment in the basement. I don't need the money to pay the mortgage, so I can save it and use it for my trips. I need to take my time and make sure that whoever I rent the apartment to is someone I feel comfortable with, someone I will enjoy having around. I want to get the back yard paved too and all of these projects are making me think that I really do have a life; a reason to get up each day.

I'm finding out things about myself I never knew. I got married when I was twenty years old, which is just ridiculous when you think about it; too young! I was so in love and it was what I wanted. Mike always took the dominant role in our relationship. For example most of our vacations were centered on the Shriners because he was a Shriner. We also went on cruises and the year before he died we went to Myrtle Beach because he was a golfer. I enjoyed the vacations because I knew he was happy and I always found a way to fit in things I enjoyed as well.

Now I get to pick what I want to do. It isn't that I don't miss him and the times we spent together, but I do enjoy making some of these decisions. All of a sudden I have no one to consider but myself. I don't have to worry about losing my home because we both had such good pensions.

My friends were always asking me to visit or go out with them. I would say yes, but later would call and make excuses for not going. I didn't want to be with people because it was just such an effort to socialize. I didn't feel like a whole person anymore. I felt like I was missing a part of myself. I sometimes find it hard to be with others who do seem whole and complete.

My friends soon figured out that my excuses were just that and began visiting me every Wednesday night. Most of the time when they arrived I was in tears and they would try to lift my spirits. I have been on sleeping pills since James died. I hate to admit that I'm dependent on them, but I know I cannot sleep without them.

It's been a long road of suffering and grief, but it does get a bit easier and I feel like I am ready to move on with my life. It's not an easy task and one that takes a great deal of effort, but I am at least ready to try.

Most of my friends are married and it's hard to find someone to do something with that does not have commitments with their significant other. I know I need to make some new friends; friends who are free to just pick up and go at a moments notice.

That first year was definitely the hardest. I tried to talk myself out of my depression by saying that I'm lucky to still have my two boys, my friends, the house and my health. I just couldn't get myself out of it and all I wanted to do was lie in bed or sit on the couch. I think it is part of the grieving process to get past that first year and all its anniversaries. I can feel that the pain is getting less and I'm looking forward to this summer and having my friends over to sit on the deck.

When I was in the Cayman Islands, I was out in the water and there was this man swimming by. He was attractive and strong and I found myself looking at him. I was surprised by that, not that I wanted to meet him, but that I was noticing men again.

I don't know if that means that I want to do anything about it. I'm independent now and I'm enjoying making decisions on my own. But it made me realize that it is o.k. to admire another man and that I wasn't disrespecting my dead husband.

I have also come to realize that although I wish Mike was still with me, I don't necessarily want to get involved with anyone right now. If I did, it would have to be a very independent man that would let me do my own thing and I can't imagine that ever happening. I don't know how things will unfold and I'm not looking, time will tell how that works out.

I don't know how my two boys would react, but I think that they would be happy for me. My mother was a widow for five years before she got remarried at age seventy-four. She is really enjoying being married again so I know it does work.

I still get the odd thing in the mail with Mike's name on it and it's hard to see. Mike was six years older than me, but his dad lived to be in his eighties. I just thought we would grow old together and that I wouldn't be widowed young. I still can't believe that I'm on my own. Sometimes you feel like you're out there on thin ice all alone and you're not quite sure what's going to happen.

I miss him and miss not having him here to love me. I miss driving home at ten o'clock at night and having him worrying that I get home safe. Someone who loved me no matter what—that's what I miss.

WORDS *of* WISDOM

TAKE THE TIME TO REALLY LEARN WHO YOU ARE.

TAKE SOME RISKS, ENJOY LIFE AND MOST OF ALL BE HAPPY.

Chapter 2

DON'T LET ANYONE ELSE MAKE YOUR LIFE DECISIONS FOR YOU

A good life is a collection of happy memories.

—DENIS WAITLEY, *The Seeds of Greatness*

It seems when you are young you have time but no money. Later in life you have money but time runs out. Death changes everything; you realize that you can't always count on what life will bring. I believe when family members are left behind they think about quality of life and helping others.

Men are programmed to provide and they feel the responsibilities. We had talked about quality of life and Dave leaving his job sixteen years ago when there was lots of work. Dave would be talking to someone that was making three or four times more money than him, but then he would think, "How can I leave my pension and severance package?" Dave didn't want to be old and not have a pension to live on. He wanted to go long haul driving because that was what he loved to do. It's a silk trap because after twenty-seven years of service you can't walk away. But in the end Dave knew that he was never going to see a cent of his pension money and that was hard for him to take. I think sometimes that Dave had more anger than anyone. He felt the kids were grown up and he was getting ready to retire and these were to be his best years and he wasn't going to see them.

Dave pulled a muscle in his back and it kept getting more painful. He went to the doctor and had some tests done. By the end of that week he was having vision problems so we went to the emergency department. When they took him in for a CAT scan they told me that they wouldn't be too long, but I had a bad feeling when they came out to tell me that they were taking more scans. Afterwards, this young doctor came in and told Dave that he had a multitude of brain tumors. Dave didn't have headaches so we never thought about tumors. They did a chest x-ray and we went back to our own doctor to look at the results. We could see that every part of the CAT scan had tumors and that the lung also had tumors. Within a week and a half it was in his liver. It was very fast, but Dave had hoped for some treatments to get a year or more. Less than a month from when Dave found out he had cancer, he was dead.

When Dave was diagnosed his main concern was that he didn't want to be in pain or be sick. I told Dave that some decisions would have to be made as there are meds for the pain and we would need to decide about treatments, but some things were decided for us because he went so quickly. We had originally gone to see what they could do for treatments but they couldn't do anything until they controlled his pain. He couldn't even sit in a wheelchair and was like a crazed animal with so much pain. They gave him medicine to keep the brain from swelling and to delay the seizures. We were going to put a hospital bed in the living room and have Extra Mural to help but Dave started seizures one night, went into the hospital and never came out.

Dave and I talked a lot when he was in the hospital. He wasn't selfish and wanted me to know it was ok to be sad. I remember saying, "As awful as I feel I want this to be the worst because I never want to lose one of our girls." Dave understood what I was feeling, but he had a way of making me feel better. He responded, "It is a different kind of pain, than if it was your child, but don't dismiss it because it is painful for you." It was a very understanding comment for him to make.

I know Dave did a lot of thinking about what would happen to him after he died. One time he asked me, "How will I know when I'm gone to the other side?" My husband was a good man so I believe he will be ok. You have to find that peace or it will drive you crazy. Dave was not a church going man but he was a man that believed. He received some relief after the Minister visited and anointed him. I think it gave him that peace of mind he was striving to find in the days before his death.

Dave died about ten minutes after our oldest daughter, Karen, got there. I was up all night thinking that every last breath was going to be his last. The first night that he had a seizure, I kept screaming at him that I wasn't ready. The following day he came back enough to talk a bit and he hung on but that would be the last time. I was thankful I got the time to say goodbye. If your husband dies from a heart attack or an accident you don't get that chance, yet at the same time I would not have wanted the six weeks of suffering to continue. It wasn't long but it was long enough to see that the pain couldn't be controlled. I wanted Dave to be at peace.

Dave and I had gotten our wills done a few months earlier, but we didn't think about preplanning our funerals. When Dave was laid out I thought that I was handling it well. I was even smiling and talking as if it was a social time to meet people I had not seen for a while, but the truth was that I was in a daze and not really taking it all in. Now I know why the sign in book is so very important, because I can't remember who was there. It was nice when people came into the funeral home and told stories about Dave. It was kind of healing to hear them.

My mother and father have done their preplanning and I can see the reasoning behind it. I did the write up for the newspaper the night before Dave died because I couldn't sleep. I knew certain things because Dave and I talked about what he wanted. I remember saying that I didn't know what I would choose for Dave to wear because he would just die if I put him in a suit. As soon as I said it I realized what I had said. He was cremated and when his ashes went out in the river everything was very organized. In the boat was the Minister, our daughters, his brother and the driver of the boat. Everyone else was on shore with me. The bag piper played *Amazing Grace* and the lay reader did the reading. We didn't tell too many people, but most of the family and all the casket bearers were there because we did it right after the funeral. My friend, Eve, found a picture of the actual river area where Dave's ashes went and I have it hanging in the house.

We decided to put a stone for him on his mother's grave. When we went in to order the stone we put his name, dates and the area where the ashes went into the river. When she entered it in the system it went off the screen and everything had to be re-entered.

When it was re-entered she asked, "Is this what you want?"

I answered, "Yes." When she hit print it disappeared off the screen again.

She looked at us and commented, "That's never happened before." We joked that Dave never knew anything about computers, but we thought he might be learning the tricks.

Driving home that same day 'On Star' came on and asked us "Can we be of assistance?" It was like Dave was talking to us. It was eerie. A few days later the bedroom lamp on his side went on and off. The new touch lamp never did it before or after that. Karen often drives without her seat belt on and Dave would haul over until she put it on. The warning for the seat beat never worked on the old car, but after Dave's death the seat belt sign started to work and continued to work until she buckled up. My hairdresser had a dream that she was at our house visiting with Dave and I.

At some point she looked at Dave and asked, "How are you?"

Dave answered, "I'm just fine". I had wanted to know if he was ok because he had suffered so much. Hearing what my hairdresser had to say gave me some peace of mind.

Our youngest daughter, Tammy, is my biggest support. Tammy was writing her exams the week he was admitted to the hospital. We found out on Sunday how bad he was and she had two exams on Monday. She had studied for them and decided to get them over with so she could concentrate on her Dad. When Tammy went to her part time job she was stressed because everyone wanted to talk to her about it. They were being nice, but it was exhausting to tell it over and over again. It made her more aware of what is really important and what is not worth worrying about. She does not have patience for people when they complain about small stuff. I often think of Tammy seeing her father seizure. She shouldn't have seen that because it's an image that she will never, ever forget. I worry about Tammy because she is dealing with her own pain plus seeing me trying to deal with my emotions.

Karen does better because she isn't here all the time. She lives away and already has a life separate from us. Karen got divorced a year after her wedding and I thought that was the worst year of my life. It's hard to look at the wedding pictures now because of mixed feelings. Karen had her father to give her away and Tammy is thinking that when she gets married she will not have her father. Karen witnessed a fatal accident before she got married. She was on her way home from university when a car passed her and went out of control. She watched one of the young men die and couldn't do anything to help him. Karen knows that she needs to talk to a professional about her father's death. I went to a professional once and if I go again I will ask him about my daughters. There may be a sense that there is something wrong with me because I needed to talk to a professional but guess what—there is something wrong. I've lost the love of my life and I need help with it. It's OK to go get help and it is good not to pretend that everything is alright when it isn't.

I was upset about Dave's death and the fact that he couldn't quit smoking. I think I was searching for things to blame and having difficulty accepting my life without him in it. The social worker told me that what I'm feeling is perfectly normal but if this is normal I wish I wasn't 'normal'. She said that I had lost my balance when I lost Dave. It makes sense that the balance is gone and that it will take me some time to get rebalanced.

This first Christmas will be hard. We haven't really gotten around to discussing it and it's almost like we are avoiding it. Half the time Dave was working Christmas Day, so Boxing Day was the day that friends and family came here. I thought of not doing it this year, but Dave would want me to do it. I have lost so much already, and it was so much a part of our life that I don't want to lose it too. Part of me is thinking that if I don't have the get together on Boxing Day then no one else will do it and that would make our first Christmas even more unbalanced.

Dave always saved out of his allowance and he would give it to the girls to get me a present. It hit our daughters that this year I wouldn't be getting a present from their father and they would not be shopping for him. I will give them some money for Christmas shopping, but it's not the same. It won't be our usual Christmas, but when you have children you have to try to make it as normal as possible.

I have a neighbour that still has his wife's ashes on the table. My Mom thinks that it's not right and that once you die you should be buried, but she isn't a widow and so cannot relate to how others may feel. Recently someone told me that I was young and that I would find someone else, but it's only been six months. I started to read this book and it talks about the dumb things people say and how to empty closets. As I read the book I thought it had been written for me. It talked about the six-month period when I thought I was on top of everything and then the bottom fell out of it. The last few weeks I've been thinking, what happened to that person that was handling everything? I'm not so busy now and it's catching up to me.

One night I got really angry because there were mice in the baby barn. I was out trying to set a trap and it was raining and windy. The door hit me from behind and it hurt. I started to yell and carry on that we didn't have that many darn mice when Dave was around. I really over reacted and it was like a release. It was like my anger was coming out in another way. I'm far too young to be a widow. I have a right to feel sorry for myself, but I am thankful that Dave was here for the girls as they grew up. We are fortunate that we didn't lose him when they were young children. There is a lot to be thankful for, but the one thing I will miss is when we have the first grandchild. Dave was so good with kids and would have been a special grandfather. I watched him last year playing with our cousin's little guy. That will be one of the hardest things to go through.

Dave was fifty-nine and I was fifty-one when he died. We would have been married for thirty years on our anniversary. I was eighteen years old when I started dating Dave so it's always been Dave and I. You go from school to being married and now years later you're grown up and on your own. Dave and I had our difficult times and money worries because I had to leave work early due to ill health. Through it all Dave was there for support and we used to discuss our decisions together. I had someone to share the blame and glory with.

On our thirtieth anniversary the only person who called me was Tammy. My mother knew it was our anniversary, but didn't want to say anything because she didn't want to upset me. My sister also knew but didn't want to call. I told them later that it hurt more not hearing from them. Every minute of that day was hard. On our twenty-fifth anniversary we had a special night away from home at a spa. I thought the thirtieth anniversary would be really special and yet when it came I had no one to celebrate it with.

On the second call home Tammy asked, "Mom, you do know what day this is?" She had thought it odd that I hadn't said anything.

I answered, "Yes, I know and it's OK."

My mother said afterwards that she didn't want to upset me, as if the hurt would go away if we didn't talk about it. When we are out together and someone starts to talk to me about Dave she will change the subject by talking about my father, who is in a nursing home. She doesn't realize that talking to others is healing and not upsetting.

We have two cats and one cat was Dave's. That cat misses him so much. Dave went outside for a smoke one Christmas Eve and found this poor cat frost bitten and hungry. He put him inside his coat and brought him in. After that, the cat would never leave him alone.

I was very surprised at the people who are hesitant to contact you following the death of your husband. A big surprise for me was my sister because she never calls me. She finds out how I'm doing through our mother because she is uncomfortable and doesn't know what to say. I have a long time friend that lost his twenty-seven year old daughter. When I talk to him now, I know he understands the loss of a loved one. Often people are there to support you at the beginning, but after a while they just fade away and you are alone once again.

I have a much better understanding of other people's pain because of what I have gone through. There will be another widow tomorrow and I will be able to relate and hopefully help her. It's an especially hard time to lose your husband when you're going through menopause. You're having enough problems with hot flashes, night sweats and mood swings without adding the stress of being a widow. Then again, it's hard to lose your husband no matter what the circumstances.

Dave and I bought the house a year after we got married and the girls planted trees in the back yard when they were young. I can't imagine not being here and I don't want to add to my stress by moving. The most important decision I made was to not make any major decisions for a while. Anything I did do would have simply been an emotional reaction in the moment and not a decision made with the benefit of time and careful thought.

I kept busy after Dave died by doing work on the house. We picked out the hardwood floors before he died and they were laid afterwards. I also did the deck because I'm thinking that I'm going to live in this house for a while. I have insurance money, widow's pension and in a few years Dave's pension will kick in. It helps that the house is paid off and there is no mortgage payment or rent. I'm very blessed that I don't have to go to work.

When I went to university I was student loan poor and had to even watch what I bought to eat. For the first time in my life I don't have to worry about money unless something really bad happens. If I want something now I simply buy it and that is not something I could have done before.

Tammy is still living here and I have no idea what I want to do in the future, but I have time to adjust before she leaves. I know she needs to move out and make a life of her own. At this time I'm thankful to have her here to watch TV and spend time with me. Sometimes she jokes that I have to be good to her because she is all I have at home. The truth is that it works for both of us because she is just finishing university.

I worry that I'm going to be lonely and my biggest fear is that I'm going to be a pathetic little soul. I don't want to feed into that fear because I don't want to create a bitter lonely life. I just don't want to be this little old lady at a coffee shop by herself.

Tammy and I miss looking over and seeing Dave in his chair watching TV. I also miss his grin and wave when he drove by someone he knew. I cried all the way through packing up Dave's clothes, but I had help from Tammy. I hope it will be less painful by the time Tammy moves out. My mother's friend said to me that it will never get better, but that is because she has chosen to live in the past. Dave would be the first to have me move on. You have to force yourself out even when all you want is to stay in and avoid people.

I look after my mother on a daily basis because my dad is in a nursing home. Mom is easy going and I think that I will have the responsibility of caring for her over the next twenty years. She stays with me every winter and I can still come and go, but in the future she will require more care. I worry that the family may think that because I no longer have a husband that I should be the only one to look after her. I stopped working years ago because of my health and they think that because I'm home I should do all the running for our parents.

I'm OK with my mother being here and she is good company, but I would like the others to kick in and do more for our parents. My advice to new widows is to not let others make those life decisions for you just because you don't have a husband. Not having a husband doesn't mean you don't have a life worth living.

I have a friend who is a recent widow and she is thinking about quitting her job. That is a big change if you have been working for a lot of years. Sometimes you get a large sum of money when your husband dies and you think you don't need to work. However, that money may not be much when it's spread over the next twenty or thirty years. I really try to resist making big decisions and reacting in the heat of the moment. I try to weigh things out carefully.

The employee assistance program through Dave's work was very helpful. Head office sent me a package with everything that I needed to fill out. My advice is to keep copies of all forms and papers because the originals I sent back got lost. If I had not kept copies I would have been in trouble. One of the things that upset me the most was that they had lost Dave's death certificate and the originals were never found. You have to be careful and only give out a notarized copy of the will and keep the original in a safe place.

Dave had said years earlier that if someone had to go, he hoped it was him. That I took care of a lot of things and he wouldn't know what to do without me. Mind you, Dave didn't realize how much I depended on him and I didn't either until he was gone. When I hear about someone who has died I think about the wife left alone. There is so much to do, so many calls to make, so much paperwork that needs filled out and no one to share the burden with.

I know that I need to join something and get out of my comfort zone. I need to be with other women to have fun. I need to talk to other widows who share an immeasurable bond of understanding and feeling. I love my family and friends, but it isn't possible to share the range of emotions I am going through with anyone but my fellow widowers.

WORDS of WISDOM

Don't let anyone else
make your life decisions for you.
Just because you don't have a husband
doesn't mean you don't have a life.

Chapter 3

STAND UP FOR WHAT YOU KNOW IS RIGHT

When one door of happiness closes, another opens;
but often we look so long at the closed door that we
do not see the one that has been opened for us.

—HELEN KELLER *1880 – 1968*

We went together all through high school and then, for two years, I would only see Jack on the weekend because he was working away from home. I recently found some old letters he had written saying that he couldn't wait till we got married and I could be with him. In one letter he said he worked on his car that night replacing a wheel bearing that cost him a whole dollar to buy. I thought that was funny and told our youngest son, Colin, about the cost because he works on cars like his father did. Colin laughed and said, "Mom, I changed a wheel bearing on a car last week and it cost me seventy dollars." Jack would get such a kick out of that if he were still around.

We were married for forty-three years and were together four years before that. It wasn't easy, but we put the effort in and made it work. I'm truly thankful that God brought us together and that I never had to work. Jack wanted me to stay home and be there for the children.

Jack was sixty-four and I was sixty-one when he died and there has never been anyone else for me. Trust was such an important part of our marriage. All those years and all of a sudden he's gone, so how do you trust someone else? When you marry young you grow up together and there is no baggage brought into the relationship. Now if I dated there would be a lot of life lived on both sides and that would make it hard.

Our daughter, Dawn, was thirty-three when she got married. The wedding was booked for the seventh of July, but she put it off until September because so much was going on. The wedding kept me going because I worked on it while Jack was sick. Dawn had picked a wedding dress out and I went to see her try it on. When I got back, Jack said to me that I should have taken a picture so he could see how she looked. He never did see Dawn in her wedding dress because he died on July seventeenth. I wish we had done a quiet home wedding when he was still with us and had the big wedding later at the church. I wanted a memorial candle for the wedding and Dawn wanted her Dad to be mentioned. We found a vase that was perfect and we put a candle in it. The Pastor suggested that we light it and have it carried in by the grandsons. I still find it peaceful and reassuring to light the candle and think about Jack.

Jack retired when he was fifty-nine because the company was cutting back and offered him a buy-out package. He worked thirty-seven years so the deal was too good to pass up. Later Jack started losing weight and sleeping a lot, but he was always working around the place so I didn't think anything about it.

One Sunday I came home from church and Jack said, "You're going to have to take me to the hospital." I asked, "Why?" Jack said he was passing blood so we went to the emergency room. They said that it was because he had been taking aspirin and not to worry about it. Later we went to our doctor, who sent him for a chest x-ray. We were told that he had asthma, which causes shortness of breath. So we didn't worry when he was working out in the garage and would get short of breath. Jack still had this pain in his back and so he went for more blood tests. Then the doctor told Jack that he had a tumor in his liver.

Jack said, "What the hell is going on, you said I had asthma and now you say I have a tumor?" The tumor grew in his liver and it was caused by a protein shortage. Jack asked the doctor about a liver transplant.

The doctor said, "The tumor has to be less than three centimeters to do the transplant and yours is eight." When I got home I went right on the Internet and looked it up. It said that there was no cure, but of course we didn't really take it in. We found out that the disease is hereditary and in order for Jack to have it both his mother and father had to have the genes. I was tested right away because we were afraid our children might have it. I don't have the genes so our children are OK but they are carriers.

Is anyone ever truly ready to die? I once asked Jack if he was ready to die and he told me that he was. Most of the time that he was in the hospital he shared a room with a Christian. When he died I believe that he understood what was happening to him and through his faith he would be OK.

The hardest part of the whole process was the last week of his life when he went into Palliative Care. Jack was peaceful and content in the hospital because even though he was in a lot of pain he felt safe there. We played a lot of spiritual music and everybody was there for him. The first day that we were there the head nurse and doctor asked to speak to me. We went into another room where they said that they didn't think that I understood what Palliative Care was for. I said that I thought I did, but they could tell me.

They said, "It's for people who can't handle it at home and to give the caregiver a rest." I understood that, but I got the feeling that they didn't want Jack there. The following day when I went in the same nurse told me that I had to take Jack home.

I questioned, "What's the difference between my husband and everyone else that is here?" But she didn't answer me and I think they wanted the bed for someone else.

I pleaded, "My husband doesn't want to go home because he feels safe here." Jack had been on morphine for the last two weeks and everyone knew his time was coming to an end.

She insisted, "You're going to have to take him home."

I replied, "Then you will have to tell him because I'm not."

She said, "I get the feeling that you think we are trying to push your husband out."

I answered, "Yes, I do feel that way."

She went into Jack's room and told him, "We are going to send you home. How do you feel about that?"

Jack was on heavy morphine and was groggy in thinking, but he answered, "I don't want to go home." She ignored him, "Well you have to go home because there is nothing we can do for you here." My biggest regret is that I did take him home. I should have put up a fight instead of giving in.

We brought him home Thursday by ambulance and he sat for a long time on the couch and didn't move much. Monday when the VON nurse came to the house, Jack had gone into a comatose state. She called the ambulance and the hospital found a bed in the heart unit for him. The next morning the head nurse from Palliative Care and the doctor came into the room to talk to me.

They asked, "Would you consider taking your husband back to Palliative Care?"

I rebuffed them, "Never. He's not going back there." He died that night in the heart unit. Palliative Care was the worst because I felt he should have been able to stay when he didn't want to go home. I don't know why they pushed him out and I can't let it go. I don't have the answer and it still bothers me to this day. He was only in Palliative Care two or three days before they sent him home. Palliative Care made him go home Thursday and he died Tuesday. I know others that have been there for months, but they couldn't keep him for a week. My family doctor said that I should go talk to someone to get some answers, but I never did.

Jack said he wanted to be cremated, but I said we aren't going to worry about that right now. I was always saying to him that I wasn't ready to face those decisions yet. The week before he died we arranged the funeral. I never thought I would think of an undertaker as a friend, but he was really nice. I didn't have Jack cremated. I think he said that to save me money not because it was what he really wanted. Jack had been so sick that I wanted an advance viewing, but I couldn't get over how good he looked.

Our grandson, Lee, really loved his grandfather because he was here every day after school. I wasn't sure how Lee was going to be at the funeral parlor. Jack did a lot with Lee and taught him how to play the piano. When people came in Lee would take them over to the casket and talk to them about his grandfather. Seeing how well Lee was doing was medicine to me. Lee bought a screwdriver and socket set and put them in his grandfather's pocket. He would touch Jack and I thought it was good because when I was young I was terrified of dead people. Lee doesn't have that fear. When Jack died our eldest son, Timmy, went to the cemetery in the area where I grew up and called to tell me there were two plots available. I found out later that my brother in-law was buried beside us and I felt it was meant to be that we got those plots.

I was back and forth many times to the tombstone company as I wanted the stone to be a lasting memorial. I wasn't originally going to put any pictures on it but Jack used to race so I wanted his car on it. Our wedding picture is on one side and his car is on the other. It also has our wedding date and our names. On the back is the family picture and all around it are pictures of family members and the grandchildren. It's not supposed to fade and around the pictures it says "Thank

You Lord for Your Blessings to Us." I put a lot of thought into the stone and it took me about six months to do, but it was worth it to me.

My sister, Kate, is a widow and because I am the youngest there have been a lot of deaths in the family. When I came home from Jack's funeral I went right to the bedroom and packed everything up. I gave it to Colin and told him to take it to charity because I didn't want it around. Kate still has some of her husband's clothing and it's been about six years. She held on and still goes to the cemetery all the time. I go to the cemetery sometimes but I don't need to go there. When the stone arrived I didn't tell anyone and I went to see it by myself. It was a beautiful day, the sun was shining and it was warm. I made sure the stone was where it was supposed to be and afterwards I went shopping all by myself.

When I got home some of the family was put out that I hadn't told anyone that the stone was in and that I was going to see it. I didn't know how I was going to react so I didn't want anyone to be there, it was my time. Colin went that night and the rest went when they wanted.

Most of my family knows God and believes in heaven, but I don't think heaven is the way we think it is. I recently went to a funeral where the Pastor read the story, "Dragonflies and Water Bugs" to the kids. It's about how the water bugs climb up and become beautiful dragonflies, but they can't come back to tell the other water bugs. That's what death is like and only some of the water bugs struggle to become dragonflies. It's a mystery and only God knows what is truly in someone's heart.

The first year after Jack died; I woke up one morning and decided that I would invite all my brothers and sisters to the house. I had one sister who was in a special care home and she wasn't happy, so I thought it would be nice for her to see everyone. Everyone came but that sister because she wasn't feeling well. It was really good medicine for me to see everyone. I took a picture of us all and I had a picture of my missing sister inserted for Christmas.

The first Christmas I went to Dawn's for dinner and that was a big change because we always had it here. It was Dawn's first Christmas with her husband and so it seemed right to go there.

Shortly after Jack died I was driving along and I couldn't stop the car because the cruise control was stuck on. I went up the hill and put the car into reverse to stop it. I didn't care what happened to the car because I had to get it stopped. That's when I felt it; the total loss of Jack because he would have taken care of all the car problems. It just hit me that he was really gone from my life. I thought, "Where are you?"

I called Colin and he said he would be right there. While I waited I found a box of tissues in the car and I just started cleaning everything inside and out. I was so high strung and scared that I called home three times and got Jack's voice mail each time. That's why it hasn't been changed because I didn't want to lose it. I thought that I'm never going to hear his voice again and I find it comforting. Jack says "Sorry can't come to the phone right now" and it seems like he is talking to me. I think I will try to get a copy of his voice. If I feel lonesome I know I can call up and hear him. It's been almost two years and his voice is still on the answering machine telling the callers to leave a message.

I have made no big changes in my life. I have thought of doing some small renovations to the house, but I can't seem to find the motivation. I feel kind of guilty because the deck in the back yard has been needing repairs and I used to say to Jack that if anything happened to him, I was going to get a new deck. Now it's been almost two years and the deck still hasn't been replaced. I have no focus anymore, but I try to stay busy. I can't see any difference as the time goes on because it has never really gotten any easier.

I had paid the cell phone bill on the wrong account, that we didn't use any more, so the money was just sitting there as a credit. When I called I got a call center and they wouldn't do anything for me because the account was in Jack's name. It had never gotten changed over. I did open a new account, but that credit is on the old account and I'm still fighting to get it back.

Dealing with the bank was easy because they knew both of us. I am really thankful that we didn't have any bills and the house was paid for. I wouldn't want to move and have to pay rent. Jack's company had life insurance for him even though he was retired and also a good pension. I didn't know how much insurance Jack had until after he died. We didn't talk about it because it would be like saying he was going to die.

I didn't know about the investments so I filed that first year without them. I had to re-file and I found it frustrating as Jack used to do all the paper work.

Even though Colin is thirty, he will always be my baby boy. I would have no problems living with him and his future wife if they stayed here. Colin has already said that if I wanted to leave the house he would like to buy it. If I stay and something happens to me it will be left to him. Colin is the last one living at home and I'm just waiting to see what he will do. For now he does all the maintenance work around the house. Colin feels like his father; that you don't pay someone when you can do it yourself.

When his father died, Colin said, "Don't worry Mom, I'm going to look after you." Jack had some valuable tools and equipment in the basement and I gave them all to Colin to work on cars like his father did. We had Tommy between Dawn and Colin, but life just seems to be hard on him. He has never been back to the gravesite since the funeral. Tommy seems to be trying lately to relate with the family. I look back and think that we did the best we could at the time and I can't change anything in the past.

While Jack was sick I thought a lot about what I was going to do on my own. I thought about my mom who was widowed at about the same age I was. My mom was in the hospital when dad walked into her room and dropped dead at the foot of her bed. He was sixty-five and had just retired. I kept thinking back to that time because they seemed old to me. I never thought of Mom as being young because she was forty-six when I was born. So I thought if my Mom can do it, then I can do it.

God did bring me through it better than I ever thought. If I didn't have faith and God it would have been so much harder to bear. God pushes things your way for a reason. I remembered that the Bible says, "That in all things ask, for I am here for you." I pray that in all things, "Your will, will be done." Our husbands are no longer in pain and they don't have to worry about paying bills or facing troubles. Jack is free and I wouldn't want to wish him back to the pain and suffering he was going through.

I was sick the summer before Jack got cancer and I had a pacemaker put in. It was hard to accept because I don't drink or smoke, but I had four brothers that died of heart attacks. The pacemaker stops my heart from racing. After Jack died I wasn't feeling well and I found out that one of my leads wasn't working. So I had to go into the hospital and have another lead added. When I was sick Jack looked after me and now I don't have anyone to do that. Colin has always been there, but it's not the same and I don't want him to think that he has to stay here for me.

I liked being married because you have someone to share the load with. I don't know what the future will hold. You do what you have to do at the time. The relationship with my children is very special and I don't know how they would react to someone new in my life. I go out to enjoy myself and my daughter is my best friend. I'm busy with the grandchildren, but the evenings are lonely.

People say, "Don't worry you will find someone else", like I had just lost a family pet instead of my husband. When you have a husband you plan to do things together, like certain yard work in the spring.

But once they are gone you don't plan things, you just do as it comes along. It's almost like you are going to die too, so you don't plan much into the future. I just can't focus on planning anything. It took me six months to decide to paint the kitchen.

Sometimes I have a lonely day and I get thinking about everything. It's an empty spot and I find that I don't like being called a "Widow". I never wanted to be alone, but I'm getting used to it. I don't dream about the future anymore. There is no "us" in my future so it's like there's no need to plan. You're alone in your heart even if you're in a room full of people.

WORDS *of* WISDOM

My advice to new widows is to
stand up for what you know is right.

Chapter 4

DON'T EXPECT
A QUICK FIX

Learn to enjoy every minute of your life. Be happy now.
Don't wait for something outside of yourself
to make you happy in the future.
Every minute should be enjoyed, savored.

—EARL NIGHTINGALE, *1989*

bunch of women just having fun, dressing up and laughing together is the most healing thing any woman can do. I joined curling shortly after my husband died. I could go curling anytime and I didn't need a partner. It was a great social outlet for me. I always had a good time and I never felt like a fifth wheel. It was very affordable for almost six months of entertainment. I could curl up to three times a week, plus go to many different weekend events.

I was only forty-six when my husband died so I had to get out. I didn't want to get into the trap of staying home. I also volunteer at the gift shop at the local hospital for two hours a week. It doesn't take a lot of time, but it gets me out and makes me feel helpful and I enjoy it.

Joseph was only forty-six when he died. I was fourteen when I started dating him, but I wouldn't recommend that now; it is just so young. I dated him for seven years before we were married. I was twenty-one when I finished teacher's college and we only had one child, Emily. My parents looked after Emily when I worked so I had it very good in the earlier years of my marriage. I worked till Emily was in grade nine.

After her ninth school year, we felt there was enough money coming in and I could stay home with Emily. Joseph worked for the city for twenty years and he loved it. I wanted to quit my job and be a stay at home Mom. Everything seemed to be working out nicely. Up to the time I was forty my life was really good, but after forty everything seemed to fall apart.

Joseph got caught up in the trouble the city was having with their union workers. As a supervisor, Joseph was held responsible for a lot of the issues. He fired someone and it came back to haunt him because they held it against him. The city fired Joseph around the same time Emily, who was only nineteen years old, got pregnant. We had a lawyer fighting to clear Joseph's name because he lost everything when he got fired, including his pension.

There was nothing big they could charge him with, but there was enough for him to never get his job back. The city always had trouble with its workers. Emily had a car and Joseph had taken it over to the city garage to have the door fixed, but that was what everyone was doing. However, they were cleaning up the city, or so they said and they used Joseph as an example. Nothing was really big and he never stole any money. Joseph loved working for the city and whenever we went for a drive he would show me all the work that was being done.

After he lost his job, Joseph got into satellite dishes. He had a little business selling and setting them up. He also had a job working on the toll bridge. Joseph had known a lot of people from working with the city and it was hard to have everyone talking about his job loss. His mother was alive at the time and it was very hard on the family. Having everything in the papers and on the news was more than unnecessary. My name was even put in the paper once. I kept it for a long time and then I threw it out because I didn't want our granddaughter to ever see it. Emily was very close to her Dad and she never accepted what had happened to him and his job. It was a very difficult time because everything that happened was in all the newspapers and our name was known to everyone. Emily had to face her friends and all the news was against her Dad.

It went to court and he was acquitted of the charges on Christmas Eve. All the fight was taken out of Joseph and he didn't want to go back to court against the city for lawyer's costs, back pay or pension. He just wanted to be left alone to move on. We had no more money to pay lawyer fees and Joseph wasn't in the union so he didn't have any protection. All this happened within five years because our granddaughter, Anne was almost five when Joseph died. It took a long time for it to go to court.

Joseph's mother was sick at the time and she was in a nursing home. She didn't like it there and he found it hard to visit her. Joseph's mother brought him up because his father died when he was young and so he was very close to her. He was the baby and he couldn't do any wrong in his mother's eyes.

At one point just before Anne was born and all the trouble happened at work, Joseph left me. When he lost his job he came back to me, but a lot of things were never resolved. There was a lot of hurt in our relationship because Joseph was a heavy gambler. He loved cards and he loved the races. Joseph had always gambled and I turned a blind eye to it because it was easier to pretend everything was alright than to fight with him. Women try to keep the peace. But I always knew he loved me and when he was sick, he needed my support and I was there for him.

We lost everything before Joseph died. He got another job, but the money wasn't as good. My mother and father never owned a home and were looking for a house to buy. The house my grandparents lived in at one time was for sale and my mother and I went to look at it. We really liked it so my mother approached my father about buying it. They never bought a house before because they didn't feel that they could afford it, even though my father had always worked for the railroad and they had some money saved. They decided to purchase the two-storey home and Joseph and I moved in upstairs. We sold our house to move in with them, but everything we got from the sale of it went to the bills and the lawyer fees. We had nothing left but our furniture. Emily and her daughter Anne, as well as her boyfriend, stayed upstairs with us for a while. After my father died, mom wasn't well so we moved downstairs to live with her. Emily, split from her boyfriend, and Anne stayed upstairs so they could have their own place.

Joseph had diabetes and didn't want to admit to being sick. He never took his condition seriously and ignored it most of the time. He often worked from morning till eight o'clock at night and did not eat right. I would chase him down to get him to take his needles and pills. Complicating matters, he was diagnosed with Lupus, a hereditary blood disorder. He just wasn't a well man.

Joseph died from a massive heart attack. Emily was around twenty-four and Anne was about five when Joseph died. It was a very difficult time, because without him there just wasn't a lot of money to live on. Joseph died in August and I stayed home one more year until Anne was in grade one then I went back to work. We were married twenty-five years when he died.

Joseph was sitting at the supper table and just dropped dead. I was at the store when he died and my mother and brother were talking to him while supper was cooking. It was a real shock because we didn't know he had any heart problems.

The funeral seemed to go on forever with people coming to see me. I put a pack of cards and a racing program in his pocket when he was laid out. It was my way of sending Joseph on his way. It was something I just wanted to do. When

Joseph died we were just getting back on our feet. Joseph's aunt died before him and left us a little bit of money. I used some of it to help pay for his funeral.

I have thought about preplanning my funeral because I want certain things done like the song played, "It's a Wonderful World." I paid about seven hundred dollars for two burial plots and now they are selling for over three thousand dollars. If I had preplanned my funeral years ago when Joseph died it would have been a lot cheaper for me.

Anne was my saving grace because I looked after her when Emily worked. It was good for me to have someone else to look after and not to be thinking of myself.

There was some insurance money and I was still staying with and looking after my mom. My two brothers came to visit when our mother was alive and got her to sign the house over to me. They made sure that when she died I would have the house to live in.

I was very fortunate that I had such good brothers and they didn't want anything from the estate. Having the house free of a mortgage was what helped get me back on my feet.

I decided to go back to teaching, but I didn't have the university teaching degree that they now wanted. I had to get special acceptance for my college papers, but I was fortunate that I was able to get back into the school system and was able to teach again.

When I quit my job to stay home with Emily, I took my pension out. I thought I wouldn't need it because Joseph had a good job with a great pension. I soon realized that I should have stayed working because I had to buy back my old pension and it took me a long time. I had to pay back both employer and employee shares, but I needed that pension.

I taught half days for one year and then I worked full time hours. I worked for the next thirteen years before I retired at age sixty. It was very hard to get people in for my mother and she didn't want me to leave her. I felt guilty, but I needed to work. In the end she went from the house into palliative care and died there.

I didn't see anyone for professional counseling, but I would tell anyone that's going through a hard time to get some help. I had a friend that went to the widow's group at the funeral home and that was very helpful for her. Women need other women to talk to. When Joseph died I had a good friend that I talked to. I didn't have any sisters so my friend helped me, but I think professional help is still good to have.

My husband lost his job, we lost our home, savings, and his pension, our reputation and then I lost him, just as things were starting to improve. I went through a lot of anger and I felt my life just shouldn't have been that way.

I belong to my church and the women's church group used to call me "Maya the Joiner" because I stayed busy. I recently moved into a senior's home and there are lots of things to do. I started walking a lot and I have gone on some trips. You can't go anywhere unless you double up because it's too expensive to go single. I still curl because it is an affordable and fun way to socialize. I volunteer helping others which gets me out to meet new people.

I went with a friend to the single's club, but I wasn't comfortable and never went back. I never felt I had to get married again. It's a standing joke between my friends and I because I have always said if I find a man he has to have a big boat to take me down south. Also, he has to have money because I'm not doing the dishes or his laundry. It was funny because the principal where I worked had a boat and tried to fix me up with this divorced man who also had a boat. I said, "No way" and it made me realize just how little I wanted to take on the responsibility of another relationship. I have good sister in-law's and my daughter for support.

I wish I had been a little more careful about the money that was left to me at the time. I went through it faster than I realized. You have to watch your finances and not make any great moves within that first year because you're not really thinking clearly, even though you think you are. When you're a widow you go pick up the insurance check and no one really takes the time to explain that if you invest this much over time you will have this much when you want to retire. So instead you take the money and fix up the house or buy a car or take a trip and before you know it the money is gone and you're left worrying about the future. You don't really realize at the time that there is no more income coming in from your husband, yet you still have to live your life.

WORDS *of* WISDOM

DON'T EXPECT A QUICK FIX.

TIME IS PASSING ANYWAY SO MOVE FORWARD

WITH A PLAN FOR YOUR FUTURE.

TAKE RESPONSIBILITY FOR YOUR LIFE.

Chapter 5

WRITE IT ALL OUT IN A JOURNAL

For things to change, you have to change.
For things to get better, you have to get better.

—FROM JIM ROHN'S *Leadership Weekend Event*

Wentered

e went on a cruise and Andrew lifted some heavy suitcases. He had some chest pain so he went to the doctor and they said that it was a pulled muscle. At the time I didn't notice anything, but looking back he was more tired than usual. Andrew was trying to quit smoking but after he died I found cigarettes in the shed and in the car. Andrew enjoyed life, he enjoyed a social drink, eating good food and socializing with our friends. Andrew wasn't just a husband, he was my best friend. He was forty-five when he died and I was forty-three. We had been married for eighteen years and had a twelve-year-old son, John, and nine year old daughter, Liz. When it happened I couldn't believe it for days, it was so surreal to me.

We were at the cottage and Andrew had gotten up to make the morning coffee. He told me my coffee was ready. I said that I'd be there in a minute. Andrew came to me and said that he was having pains in the chest. Immediately I said that we should go to the hospital.

Andrew agreed, "Yeah, maybe I should, but I think I'll just go lie down for a minute." As soon as he lay down he began to convulse. Andrew was gone in seconds. I knew he was dead because his eyes were open, but nothing was there. Liz was in the other bedroom and she heard me calling out to him. She asked me what was wrong and I told her to go get our neighbor and to stay there. The ambulance came and did CPR, but I knew it was too late. Telling Liz what happened to her daddy was one of the hardest things I've ever had to do.

We had just taken John to summer camp the day before. I called the camp and told them what happened and that I would be there in about an hour and a half. They said they wouldn't tell him anything, but they would bring him to the office. As soon as he saw me he freaked out and asked what's wrong. I told him that we had to take Dad to the hospital in the morning. John asked me if his Dad had died and I had to tell him yes.

It took me a while to be able to say it. I just couldn't speak the words. John was pacing like he just wanted to get out of his own skin; he had been so close to his father.

John and Liz both went through it, but they did it differently. I don't know if it's a gender thing or the difference in their ages. Liz was all about, "Where is Dad now and is he alright?" John was concerned about how we would manage as a family without Dad. He worried about the house and who would change the oil in the car. In the days that followed, people kept saying to John that he was the man of the house now.

I said, "You are not a man, John, you are a boy, and don't ever think that you have to be the man of the house. I'm your mother and I will look after what needs to be done." It took him a while to understand that he wasn't responsible for the family.

At the funeral parlor, I wanted to see Andrew before the kids did to make sure he looked OK. I looked at him and he looked handsome with his suit on. People were coming in and saying how good he looked. It was obvious by everyone's comments that he was very well liked. They were telling me stories of things he had done for others that I hadn't been aware of. It made me feel good and I was proud that he had been my husband.

The children wrote letters to their father and put them in the casket. John's letter said, "It was almost like you knew what would happen because you taught me so much. Now I can help Mom." Liz's letter talked about her love for him and how she would miss him.

When we were leaving the funeral parlor I asked, "Where's Andrew?" Then I thought 'Oh my God', look what I just said.' I was so used to having him beside me. It was like a bad dream and I thought I would wake up and everything would be the way it was before.

I bought the most expensive casket in the whole place, made out of mahogany. Andrew would have killed me, but I wasn't thinking it out. Andrew loved oak and later I thought, 'Why didn't I get an oak casket?' Everything had to be the biggest and the best to show that I loved him. You can't second-guess decisions made, it is what it is.

John really wanted to do a reading at his father's funeral. I had a backup in case he changed his mind that day, but he got up and did it. The church was packed and I don't think there was a dry eye in the place. I think doing the reading made him feel like he was part of the service. Later I gave John his father's good watch and high school ring, which he treasures to this day.

The stress caused me to lose thirty pounds, but my health stayed fairly good. My sisters were excellent and my mother was amazing in her support, but my father was a disappointment. He was a typical man from a different generation who didn't want to talk about it. He just told me to" buck up" and "It's all water under the bridge." He wasn't saying it to hurt me. He felt he was helping me to face the reality, but that wasn't what I needed to hear from him. My brother, Tim, was worried about me. He would come over if anything needed to be done around the house. He drove me to the cottage to get Andrew's clothes out and to prepare the cottage for the winter.

Tim asked me, "Are you going to cry?" He didn't want me to cry because he didn't know what to do if I did.

I answered, "I don't know, but I'll try not to." I did cry, but he took me anyway and we got through it.

I went back to work four months later; it was the middle of November. I only worked four days a week for the rest of the year. I felt that I couldn't hold myself together any longer than that. Even then I sometimes didn't make it, and I would go down to the school furnace room and bawl my eyes out. I brought makeup to work with me to repair the damage I would do if I cried. The janitor was great because he would come in and not say anything, he would just sit there with me. One day he gave me a sucker because he didn't know what to say or do. It showed me that he cared and that was all that was needed. The rest of the staff was very supportive and bent over backwards to help me.

I did not make any major decisions that first year. I was very busy with the children, looking after them and driving them where they had to go. That was good because I didn't have too much time on my hands.

I took a course at the funeral parlor to help me through the grieving process. I went through all the stages of grief—the anger, the bargaining and the denial. After going through all the stages things got better with time, but as I look back I remember thinking that I was managing, but in truth I wasn't doing well at all. I remember breathing into Andrew's bathrobe to get his smell and to feel that connection.

I asked John and Liz to make cards for their father that first Father's Day. I reminded them that he was still their father and that he will always be their father. We have a special memory box and that was where they put their Father's Day Cards that year. We also have a special memory candle that we light for every occasion, like Christmas and their graduations.

I didn't cook a Christmas dinner that first year. I said to John that we didn't need lights outside, but he wanted them. So at twelve years old, he was outside putting up the Christmas lights. It broke my heart to see that little boy in the cold struggling to get the lights up. When you have little children, you have to put your feelings aside sometimes. In fact, it is a blessing because it helps you carry on.

When we got married, Andrew was sick and we didn't go on our honeymoon. Because of that, every anniversary we would go on a trip even if it was just a weekend away with my sister watching the kids. We never missed an anniversary. On that first anniversary, just days after his death, I went to the cemetery and there was just dirt and dead flowers there. I stood at his graveside and said, "This isn't what I'm supposed to be doing today." We had planned to be out on our boat and I'm standing there talking to myself.

I said, "I don't even know if you can hear me." As I spoke there was a gust of wind that came and blew my hat off. I didn't think anything of it. I went and picked up my hat and put it back on. As I stood there, I suddenly realized that there wasn't even a breath of wind in the air. I have faith and felt that Andrew was there with me and, yes, he could hear me.

One night I dreamed that he touched me. I felt his hand on my hip and I knew that it wasn't possible, but I didn't care. I thought, I'm just going to enjoy the feeling and I drifted off to sleep. No one will ever tell me that he wasn't there with me. Someone told me once you can feel their presence, and that they will stay close to you as long as you need them. Once they know that you're alright, they will leave and rest in peace.

My dreams at that time were about what I was feeling, but I wasn't actually realizing or acknowledging the feelings of abandonment. I had a dream that I went to our neighborhood and the house was gone or I would dream that I was looking for Andrew and I couldn't find him anywhere. In another dream, we were on a cruise and he wouldn't dance with me. Those were all dreams that were symbolic to me. I had those kinds of dreams for the first year and then they stopped.

I kept the boat for about four years because I didn't want to make any drastic changes. I used the boat, but I didn't like driving it. When John turned sixteen he wanted to take it out himself and it was then that I said it was time to sell it. I haven't seen it on the river, but if I did I would have a sense of loss. I still have the cottage and I try to keep things the same for the kids. I tried to keep everything the same, looking after the house, cottage, boat and car. It was a lot of work and worry. I had a full time job and I tried to do it all. I tried to do what two people used to do and after a while I realized that I should let up on myself. I said to myself, 'Ruth, you don't have to open the cottage up on May the fifteenth every year just because that was the date we had always done it. Give yourself some slack, if it is a little later its OK.'

I don't mind being at the cottage on my own, but after a while it gets lonely and empty. It's a big expense and a lot of work keeping up the cottage and the house. I used to cry every time I had to mow the grass or shovel the driveway.

Thirteen years later I still get mad because I think it isn't fair. Just last week when I was stacking wood in the backyard the lady next door was coming back from shopping. Her husband is helping her bring in the bags and I'm out there doing the work that Andrew would have been doing. There is this part of me that feels resentment that I'm doing it all on my own.

Our couple friends slowly disappeared and that was very disappointing. A lot of times men are very uncomfortable around a widow and so my social life changed a lot. We had a really close couple that we would go out with, but it was different after Andrew died. I felt that I was gradually left behind by our couple friends. It is then that you realize that you have to make new friends and live your life differently.

There were times after Andrew's death that I would feel guilty for laughing or having fun. Many people don't know that even when you're laughing, you can still be full of pain inside. Sometimes they hurt us with their comments, but they don't mean it. Until you go through it you don't really know what it feels like. The difference between a widow and a non-widow is empathy; a fellow widower understands where a non-widower feels sorry for you.

My life is not the way I want it to be because I would like to have someone to share it with. About four years after Andrew died I was introduced to a really nice man. We dated for two years and I thought that he was the right man for me. The children didn't react well to it and in the end it didn't work out because he was jealous of my son. I tried to explain to him that it wasn't like I have a cup of love to give, and that I give three quarters to my son and one quarter to him. It is two separate and different loves, but he couldn't understand that. I told him that if I had to choose between him and my son, I didn't even have to think about it—it would be my son. Later I realized that he wasn't at all the man that I had thought he was.

I know if I meet someone and we live together that it wouldn't be an easy adjustment. I think it would be really hard to share my space after thirteen years. Sometimes I go to bed and think how nice it would be to have someone to hold me and other times I think how nice it is to have the whole bed to myself. Andrew and I had a great relationship and I'm not going to settle for anything less than great. I must admit though that it gets lonely at times.

By the time the children grew up I had become more accustomed to being on my own. I encouraged them to go ahead and have lives of their own. John is an engineer in New Zealand and Liz is moving away to attend university. I am very proud of my children and I believe that because of what we have been through we have an extra special bond.

Things change over the years and in a lot of ways it gets better, but there are missing pieces that I would like to have back. You have to work yourself through it all, and the only way to do it is to give yourself the time that is needed. I've had many girlfriends who have helped me a lot. One in particular had lost her husband a few years earlier; and she was the one who helped me the most. My other friends were great, but they didn't understand like she did. There is no doubt in my mind that it takes a widow to really understand another widow's feeling.

I was a teacher for thirty-two years and retired at fifty-one with a good pension. Since my retirement a lot of great things have come my way. I had a lot of short term, fun jobs that were gratifying to do. A representative of Oscar De La Renta asked me if I wanted to do demos. All I had to do was promote the product. I love to dress up, I love perfumes and people so this opportunity was right up my alley. I did that for a couple of years.

Later, the Chanel district manager approached me and I did that for a few years. It was a lot of fun. I also got involved in election work and I loved the challenge. Never in my dreams had I thought that I would be doing that kind of work, but it had just fallen into my lap. You don't know the path that life will take you. I hope that by telling my story, it will help another widow to see the opportunities that may come her way if she is open to it.

I read a book entitled "Why did Daddy die?" and I was convinced the whole book was about me. A few months after Andrew died I sold his car and the book talked about that very thing. Watching the car go out the driveway was another part of my life going away. Piece by piece, I was losing so much of what had been the fabric of my life. In the book the author talked about how you may feel about certain things that happen and the questions that children ask. In the book "I Can't Stop Crying", there are many different stories about the loss of loved ones. These books were of great benefit to me. I read a lot of those kinds of books in the first couple of years.

After Andrew died, I called the Catholic Diocese and asked the secretary if there was anything available to help widows and she told me that there was United Singles. Stupidly I asked her what that was. She explained that it was a single's club to meet men. I told her, that's not what I'm looking for as my husband has only been dead a few months. I was looking for advice and support. The support group through the funeral home was of great help. At one time there were as many as twenty-five women. One night I looked around the table and noticed that they were all young women. They were in their thirties, forties and fifties. One was in her twenties. Everyone is so different and their situations are different as well, but one thing is for sure, it hurts like hell. It will hurt for some time, but as time passes you will feel better. The person who can help the most is someone who has gone through it, and that person is another widow. Meet other widows and get their advice and help. Later I helped a friend deal with his loss. By having done that I felt I had given back what I had received years ago.

I bought a beautiful hard-covered journal on the advice of a friend. At first I thought, "What will I write?", but once I put pen to paper my heart just poured out as I wrote. Later on I could go back and see the progress I made. I still journal a lot and it has been very therapeutic to go back and see where I have been in comparison to where I am at the time I reread it.

It was healing as my feelings rushed out, almost like a pressure valve releasing my pain and confusion. Women are resilient though, and all of it makes you stronger and helps you appreciate people and life in a different way.

WORDS *of* WISDOM

HEALING IS WHATEVER TIME IT IS—
DON'T LET ANYONE RUSH YOU.
TAKE THE TIME TO WRITE IT ALL OUT IN A JOURNAL.

Chapter 6

DON'T BE AFRAID OF REMARRYING

*The toughest thing about the power of trust is that
it's very difficult to build and very easy to destroy.*

—T. J. WATSON

I always had outside interests, but I didn't work while the children were home. After the children all moved out I went to work for five years. When the new house was being built I didn't know if I wanted to move out of the city, but we agreed that we would try it for one year. When Ryan and I moved to our new house I stopped working. We rented out our old house for that first year, but after we moved I got settled in and was happy. I started to go to the local church and I joined the women's choir and senior's group. We moved out here about fifteen years ago when I was sixty-four and I'm seventy-nine now.

We arranged both our funerals years earlier before he got sick. We did it so we wouldn't make any emotional decisions. You go through so many different emotions; fear, pain and being lonely when someone dies. I felt fear the most—'Oh my heavens, what will become of me, will I be able to keep the house, keep the fires going?' I had been married fifty-five years and all the children were grown up so the house was empty when Ryan died.

It all started when Ryan got pneumonia and then we found out that he had lung cancer. Ryan was a smoker and a heavy drinker. When Ryan was diagnosed they had him in for radiation treatments. I had asked them if the treatments would give Ryan any extra time.

They told me, "No, but it will keep the pain down and stop it from spreading." It was six months from the time we found out about the lung cancer till he died.

I wasn't aware if there were any documents to help me out at the funeral parlor. I wasn't looking around and so I didn't notice anything there. I had prearranged the funeral so it was all taken care of when Ryan died. All I had to do was go in to pay the bill and so I never talked to anyone or was offered any help. I remember that the one thing I had to do was decide on the eulogy for the funeral.

Ryan was seventy-five and I was seventy-four when he died. I had never been on my own and I was afraid of having an empty house. I have two daughters that live out of town that came to the funeral. One daughter stayed a little longer and that was a big help to me. When I went out it was a horrible, horrible feeling coming back into the empty house. I had an alarm system installed and it made me feel safer. I was always going places and having my friends in and that was what kept me going. I was always 'a doing and a going.'

We had our ups and downs in the marriage. We had nine children and lost one boy. Part of me died when my son, Stan, died as he was only twenty-one when we lost him. You cannot compare the death of a husband to the loss of a child. My heart still aches for Stan and it has been more than thirty years.

Ryan started drinking more when Stan died. I felt some relief when Ryan died because there was no joy in our relationship. Ryan had worked thirty-two years at the city's shipbuilding dry-dock and he was a great provider. However, there was a certain amount of relief and regret when it was all over because Ryan was verbally abusive. I felt guilty that I did feel relief when he was gone. I looked after the finances, meals and kept a good home. Now that I'm older I think about our life together, but I realize that you can't go back. I decided that I didn't want to carry the anger inside me any longer. I didn't want the burden of the pain. I spent a lot of time away from home, singing club, art classes, etc. and that helped me cope with the marriage. I continued with these hobbies after Ryan's death.

At first I was worried because I wouldn't have his income to support me. I thought that I might not be able to keep the house. We had insurance and he had a pension and that was a God's blessing to me. I was able to get that money along with my old age pension. He had a work insurance policy that was his even when he retired and it was three thousand dollars. We had three grandchildren in university so I gave each of them a thousand dollars. I was happy to do that because I was proud of them.

I remember when I was told that Ryan had lung cancer. He had no hearing so he didn't really understand what the doctor was saying. Our daughter was with us and we were in shock. Ryan suffered and I had to look after him and comfort all our children. I had to be the stronger one with no one to comfort me. You convince yourself that everything will work out and you have to go along with your life. I would get in the car and go for drives to cheer myself up.

Ryan stayed at home instead of the hospital and he slowly died there. The treatments did cut down his pain and they didn't have any side effects. One of my daughters suggested that I needed a weekend break and that I should go visit another daughter that lived away. Our oldest daughter came to stay with Ryan for that weekend.

When I told him that I needed a break he lectured me, "You better hope that I'm still alive when you get home." My daughter took me to a spa and I had a really wonderful weekend. When I came home there was an oxygen sign on the window. I knew at once that he had gotten worse and had to go on the oxygen to breathe. We put a bed in the living room and Extra Mural came in to help me look after him. It was less than a week from when I came back that he died. I was glad that my daughters could see how tired I was and how badly I needed that weekend break. It helped recharge me for when I got back home.

We had preplanned our funerals about two years before he got sick. We had our burial plot and tombstone. We made low monthly payments on the burial plan and the insurance covered the balance due when he died. Don't leave the decisions for your children because they will be grieving and may not think things through. It is a lot to ask of your children in time of stress to think about everything that has to go into planning a funeral. They may miss something and feel bad about it afterwards. They may also make bad decisions based on cost because they don't know your finances as well as you do.

The children have already laid claim to the things that they want. I tell them to put their name on the bottom of it so that the others will know that they have already spoken for it. We have seven daughters and one boy. How do you get seven girls to agree—you don't, so when I made the will there is an uneven number so that any disagreements can be broken.

Years ago Ryan had a heart condition and he had his heart repaired. He never went back to work after that. I hated having him home because I couldn't do my housework when he was under foot. Every once in a while he would go out or the girls would take me out for the day. Ryan and I didn't go out together because he would embarrass me with the way he would talk and treat me. I would drive Ryan to the Legion on Friday nights and leave him there. He would call me to get him when he wanted to come home. When I went to pick him up he wouldn't come because he wasn't ready. I would go back home and when he called again

I would tell him to find his own way. There were a lot of mind games. He had a girlfriend when we had only four children. I stayed because he was a worker and where would I go? Back then the women didn't matter as much; you had to put up with it. When he stopped running he never admitted it. I knew when it was over and I said to myself that I would put it behind me. But it was always there and I never could forget it.

Years later he asked me if I wanted to know about the girlfriend, but I said, "No." I should have let him talk about it because confession is good for the soul and he probably wanted to clear it off his conscience. He wanted to talk about it, but I didn't want to hear it.

When we found out how sick he was the children came up more often to see him. Ryan was their dad no matter what and they cried for him. At the funeral a friend of mind came in and I broke down and cried. That was one of the few times I cried and it was because she had lost her husband and I knew that she understood me. We never went anywhere as a couple so I didn't feel that loss when he died.

I was looking at Ryan and I saw the life go out of his eyes. I stayed there looking at him until the man from the funeral parlor came from town. The nurse called them, but I don't remember who called the children. The funeral people asked me to go downstairs while they took Ryan out of the house.

The guest book at the funeral home was wonderful because it helped to remind me of who came to pay their respects. You think you're handling it, but you're really not. Everyone handles it differently, but there are problems in doing something too soon and regretting it. I was worried about keeping the house, but I was told not to do anything for a while. Now I say, thank goodness, I didn't sell the house and that I did wait it out.

I had a financial advisor who was an insurance agent and he advised and helped me with the paper work. I didn't want everyone to know my business. When I got Ryan's life insurance I traveled a lot. My children supported my decisions and told me to have fun. They told me to not dare save it and to have no regrets. My advisor helped me with what I did want to save. I was very fortunate financially because we had insurance and had preplanned the funerals.

Once I was on my own, the children were my biggest support. When I broke down to cry it was my son that I turned to. Ryan's side of the family never kept in touch and after fifty-five years they dropped me like a hot potato. The children on that side still call me Aunt when they see me in the mall, but they have never kept in touch.

My sisters had their own husbands and didn't understand. They were not there for me, but my youngest sister did keep in touch. We started golfing together and had fun until she died at the age of sixty-three.

Ryan loved me in his way, but he wouldn't say that he loved me. Ryan would want me to say that I loved him, but as the years went by I wouldn't say 'I love you' to him. It was all very sad. I kept some of his stuff like the little items that he had in his wallet; a picture of me when I was pregnant with our first child, for example. Strange because it meant something to him, but he couldn't express it.

I had a friend come to the house when Ryan was sick. She said there was no sense talking to him and so she talked to me. It helped having someone to talk to because you don't want to talk to the children; after all he is their dad. Talking to the Minister was good for me and the doctors understand our feelings, so we can also go get unbiased help from them. We just have to ask for the help we need. I always kept it to myself, but the children knew how he treated me and would often stick up for me.

The first Christmas without Ryan I went to town and bought a fake Christmas tree with lights attached. It makes life easier because a real tree is a lot of work. The children came for Christmas and we had Christmas dinner like we always had. Afterwards they went home and the house was empty. I felt a little bit let down. Even before Ryan died I would feel lonely after all the children left. He had no hearing and wouldn't take lip reading classes so there was no interaction between us.

I was a widow for a little over a year when I started seeing Burt and about two years later we married. When I married Burt he gave his two grown children his house and he moved in with me. I was seventy-seven when I remarried. I met Burt when I went to bingo and I remember thinking what a big heart he had. At first it was just a nice friend to share things with, but the feelings were developing and eventually he asked me to marry him.

I said, "No way am I ever going to get married again." I had enough of that and was not interested in doing it again. I was determined after fifty-five years of marriage to Ryan to never get married again. But Burt convinced me by courting me and showing me how much he loved me. Burt would come to pick me up for dinner and he would be all dressed up in a suit and tie. It was so nice to be courted and treated with love. We would laugh all the time. The first marriage hadn't been the best, but I got comfortable with the idea of getting married again.

The children were happy to see me with someone and not feel responsible for me. It's only fair that they shouldn't have to look after me. They saw me on my own and not quite happy and so they were pleased to have Burt in the family. We have been married over two years and we have travelled a lot. It's good to have someone who really loves me. It is inspiring that two people can find themselves later on in life. You're not going to find a new love if you stay in and feel sorry for yourself. My daughters used to say, "Come on out, it's not the age that matters it's the attitude."

After I got married again the children stopped calling all the time because they must have felt I didn't need them. I'm never home as we are always out and about. The children are always teasing me that they have to make an appointment to come visit because we are always running the roads.

Burt wants me with him all the time and that can be hard because I'm very independent. It was a little hard getting used to having someone under my feet after being single for two years. We have different tastes and like to do different things. I like to party but he is quiet and I like to dance but he doesn't. When we go dancing, my girls will get me up to dance and that works. You have to realize that there isn't one couple that doesn't have their differences.

I was an independent woman so if I ever felt lonely I would jump in the car and go for a drive. I know I could handle being alone again if I should lose my second husband. I would be very sad, but I would survive.

I'm going to be buried between Ryan and our son. My second husband will be buried with his first wife. This is for the kids so that they will see their mom and dad in the same site.

I would tell other widows to get out and be amongst other people as often as you can. Force yourself to move on because if you don't you will get in a rut and get depressed. Your children don't want to see you like that. It's a bit selfish to have too much of a pity party.

We all have our own different feelings. You just thank God for the years that you do have. Married life is not perfect and so it can be a rough ride. When you lose a spouse early in a marriage it can cripple you, but older women also think that their lives are over. That's not true, just get out there and enjoy life. You're as lonely as you want to be. I didn't become more social, as I was very social anyway. Ryan never stopped me from going out. He was not controlling in that way.

The happiest time of my life was when all the kids were living at home and I had no time to think. I always had a grandchild visiting and now everyone is grown up. No children or grandchildren around. I would teach my grandchildren to cook and they would just love it. They would go out with bottles to collect fireflies. There are so many memories. The time is right because at this age I wouldn't be able to accept all that noise and activity.

The last grandchild is fifteen years old and I still have a cloth diaper here from when I babysat him. I am a bit of a packrat, but I've started to clean out the closets. I have four bedrooms and they used to be all filled with children and grandchildren, but now they aren't used. So I'm taking one of the bedrooms and making it into a hobby room. I'm giving things to the children that I'm not using.

Burt helps around the house, sweeps the floors and does the dishes. You're married till the rest of your days and I advise widows to take their time. I think a good marriage is about compromise and things should not be done quickly and without thought. I was very lucky at my age to find someone to love.

WORDS *of* WISDOM

DON'T BE AFRAID OF GETTING REMARRIED.
IT CAN BE EVEN BETTER THE SECOND TIME AROUND.

Chapter 7

TRY LIFE ON YOUR OWN BEFORE YOU GET INTO ANOTHER RELATIONSHIP

When you come to the end of your rope...
Tie a knot and hang on.

—FRANKLIN D. ROOSEVELT

G rant and I knew each other ten years before we got married. It was an on again, off again, relationship but then we finally got married and enjoyed it until he died. We met originally because his kids and mine were in speed skating together. We started talking at the rink and became friends. When we met each other we were both married to other people, but our marriages were not going well.

Grant drank a lot and even though my husband and I split up, I couldn't stay with Grant when he was drinking. About three years after I separated from my husband, I started going out with other men and it was about that time when Grant went to rehab and stopped drinking.

My daughter, Hannah, always loved Grant and she would bring him to the house to visit. One day, I was in the kitchen and he kissed me. It was like no other kiss I've ever had. He said he loved me all the time we had known each other. Grant really courted me and made me believe that this was it. I was forty-four when we got married by the Justice of the Peace. We had one hundred and fifty guests and an open house party to celebrate our marriage.

Years later we were in the car and he was having a lot of problems with his breathing. We went to the hospital and the doctor on duty told us that everything looked perfect.

I said, "I would like a cardiac work up done on Grant." The tests were done and after they were looked at the doctor came to see us.

He told us, "It looks like Grant has had a heart attack, but I don't think it's too bad."

They admitted Grant to the hospital.

Another doctor came in and stated, "I'm sorry, but he only has about six months to live."

Just like that everything changed. Grant had at least six to eight heart attacks and his heart was very diseased. The heart specialists told us that there was only a thirty percent chance for survival if they operated. We didn't want to settle for only six months when he could get three to five years if he survived the heart surgery.

Grant's three daughters were not happy with our marriage, but we tolerated each other until he got sick then I just couldn't tolerate them anymore. As an alcoholic, he did a lot of emotional damage to his marriage and family, and I think they felt that they had missed a lot of time with him. Now that he was sober they wanted him all to themselves. When they had a family get together they would make me feel unwelcome because they wanted all his attention.

Grant was going to surgery at eight o'clock in the morning when his three girls came to see him. One daughter was the spokesperson for them.

She asked, "Dad, can we go to a private room to talk?"

They went off and I thought they were going to tell him how much they loved him and how much he had changed in the last fifteen years. He had really tried to make it up to them for their lost childhood. When they came back I could tell he had been crying. He had a letter with him that the girls had given him. Grant just got back in time to go into surgery, so we didn't have a chance to talk.

Grant came home and he was doing wonderful so I thought I would go for a few weeks to visit my sister. My sister suggested that I ask his three daughters to look after him so I could have a break. His daughters said they were too busy. Hannah was grown up by then so she came to look after him. I think part of the problem was that Grant was very close to Hannah and his daughters were jealous. Before I left I noticed he had a little cut in his foot, but Grant said it was nothing. I was only away about a week when Grant called to say that he had dropped a can of cat food on his toe and it didn't look right. I told him to go see the doctor, but he didn't. So another couple of days went by and he called to tell me that the other foot had also turned a bad color. I told him I was coming home and I came home at once. I took him to the emergency department four times, but they kept sending him home.

On the fourth visit a doctor told us, "We have to get him to see some specialists right away because I think he's going to lose that leg."

The specialist came in and explained, "I might be able to do surgery, but it would be about four and a half hours and your heart would not take it. So I'm going to amputate the leg because amputation is only an hour and a half."

Grant was in so much pain there wasn't any other choice, so they took off his leg below the knee. I didn't think that first twenty-four hours he was going to make it.

Grant had his surgery in July and when he was in the hospital doing rehab I decided to clean up our room. I came across the letter his daughters had given him and I read it. Up to that point I had taken almost total care of him with my daughters Hannah and Jane. The letter said, "Dad we love you, but we will never forgive you for what you did." He was going into heart surgery and had a slim chance of even surviving. They gave him this letter just before he went in! After that I didn't make any effort where his girls were concerned. One thing I didn't like was Grant's relationship with his daughters. No matter what, he would always take their side. They were always having family birthday parties and Grant's birthday came around and there was no talk about a party. Grant said he was going out for a while and it turned out that they had a party for him and he was told not to bring me. I felt that he was disloyal to me, but he was stuck in the middle.

On December the nineteenth we had been out shopping and he started leaning on the car. His face had gone purple and he couldn't breathe, but then he started to breathe and feel better so we just came home. Grant went to his AA meeting that evening and when he came home he said that he was really tired and was going to bed.

When I went to bed he was sound asleep, but about seven in the morning I woke to him gasping for breath. He took a couple of gasps and died. The doctor told Grant, just days before, to enjoy each day because of his heart being so bad. I was a registered nurse's assistant so I could look after him, but because of the lost leg he couldn't do cardiac rehab to strengthen his heart. Grant died about three years after his leg was taken off.

Grant had preplanned his funeral and had written down that at the funeral his ex-wife could be there for his girls. I didn't mind his three girls with their mother because Grant wanted it, but they all stood on one side of the reception line and I was on the other side with my children. I felt they should have stayed in another part of the room and left the reception line to me. I was married to him for the last ten years and nursed him for over three of those years.

I had a lot of anger and resentment for Grant's three girls. He loved those girls and they could have made his life a lot easier, but they didn't try. I told them on many occasions that their father was very ill. Emotions were running high at the funeral parlor and I felt like kicking them all out. I didn't want to upset Grant's funeral so I put up with them.

When we went to the gravesite, we were on opposite sides of the burial plot and I prayed for peace. I looked over at the girls and I thought I lost a husband, but they lost their father so I went over to them and hugged each one. I told them how sorry I was that their father was gone.

The weight of the anger and resentment just lifted off of me. You would not believe how good that felt to me. As I hugged each girl I could feel the resentment leave me and by the time I hugged the last girl I was free of it all. It was completely gone. They didn't have peace, but I did.

I told them that there were some things that their father wanted them to have. I gathered everything together and called one of his daughters. She came to get the stuff and as she was leaving she turned to me. She asked me why I never told them how sick their father was.

I said, "You know what, I want you to go home and think about this. Do you know how many times I begged you to go to the hospital to visit your father?" After his daughter picked up the stuff I never heard from them again. Grant would never stand up for himself because he felt that he deserved it. I would speak up on his behalf when they hurt him and that was what caused the problems between us.

We had to re-mortgage the house to get it remodeled for Grant's power chair. We couldn't get mortgage insurance because of his health. The first leg was very expensive, but we had help from the War Amps program. The loans were also for a new leg that he got three weeks before he died. Grant had requested that if something were to happen to him that he wanted the leg to go to 'Doctor's Without Borders'. When I went in to see them they looked at me and said that it was meant to be because some of their doctors were leaving on Monday for Africa and would sure appreciate having it. Can you imagine that?

I got the number of Grant's pension office and they made an appointment for me to come see them. There was forty thousand in his pension plus I received the survivor pension. I have a small pension of my own and when I sold the house I had some money left after all the bills were paid. I'm a lot better off than some widows so I'm very thankful that I don't have to worry. I don't owe anything and so whatever money I have coming in is free and clear. Grant and I took an insurance policy from the Orange Lodge that was enough to cover our funeral expenses.

Grant died on December the twentieth and was buried on the twenty-third. All the presents were wrapped and the decorations were done. One of our couple friends came to the funeral and on the way home they stopped in at the house to visit. We always exchanged Christmas presents and when they came to the house it was to ask me for Grant's present back, if you can believe that. I will never forget it because when the funeral was over I was home feeling upset and it was nice to see them. I was sitting there by myself thinking that tomorrow was Christmas Eve. I was thinking all kinds of crazy things when the knock came to the door. It was just so good having them care enough to come to visit.

They said, "We came for our gifts."

I replied, "We already exchanged the gifts."

They looked at me and explained, "No, we came for Grant's gift." So they took his gift and left. I haven't seen or heard from them since. To ask for his gift back seems so cold and we had been friends for years. I just gave it back to them.

I went up to Hannah's for Christmas dinner and everyone was crying. We shouldn't even have bothered because it was awful. On the way home I was so depressed I thought about committing suicide by going down the hill and over the bank. It was terrible coming home to the empty house.

Grant's birthday was in January and so on that date I invited all the family out. We had a big pizza party and I bought a birthday cake for him. Christmas had been so bad that it felt good to do something with the family.

Most nights from January to May, I would sit in his chair, and my friend, Martha, would come to visit and we would eat chocolate every night. I used to wear his pajamas to bed and that way I felt close to him. The smell of him would calm me and it helped me to go to sleep at night. He used Old Spice and I loved that smell. I did it for a good year before I stopped. When Grant died I stopped living. I just sat in his easy boy chair and I couldn't get myself moving.

Later I realized why I was having such a hard time moving forward. I felt a lot of guilt because our relationship had changed from husband and wife to patient and nurse. When Grant died I felt guilty that part of me was tired of looking after him. I loved him, but I was worn out.

For the first six weeks after Grant died I went to see his doctor at least twice a week. He took the time to talk to me for a good half hour at least. I would come out of his office crying my eyes out and yet the next time we would go all over it again. He was extremely supportive while I worked through my grief. Doctors usually don't have the time, but I would go over every detail of Grant's death every time I went to see him. It's different when they die at home instead of the hospital. I would lie on the floor covered in a quilt where Grant had died. I got pills to help me go to sleep and once I went on them I never went off them.

I had a support system because I had Hannah and my good friend, Martha. Martha was there every day after Grant died and after we talked a while I would get tired and go lay down for a few hours sleep. She would stay and I knew the house wasn't empty. I don't know what I would have done without her comfort. I couldn't function so one day my daughter, Jane, suggested that both Hannah and I go see a counselor. I went in February and it helped me to talk about everything. He advised me not to do anything for a year so I waited until that year was over before I cleaned out Grant's clothes and personal stuff. Then in May, Hannah moved in with me and I didn't have the empty house anymore.

About a year and a half later I started to go out with Luke. Luke was so set in his way and extremely old fashioned. I loved his boys and they were good to me. Hannah had moved out by then and I was back to an empty house.

Luke asked, "I'm paying so much for rent, why don't I move in and we will split everything and get married in a little bit?" Luke moved in with me in August and we would go to darts and visit with friends. Luke introduced me to his brothers and sisters and they were good to me when we were dating, or so I thought. But it all came down to money when Luke died.

What bothered Luke's brother, Brad, was that Luke's insurance policy and one of his pension plans was put in my name. Luke filled out the insurance policy at work after he moved in with me. I didn't even know how much the insurance was until after Luke died.

Luke was overweight and he wouldn't go walking with me. He wouldn't go get another opinion on his blood pressure because he had total faith in his family doctor. Whatever the doctor said Luke trusted without questioning. I believe the patient has accountability for what happens to them. You can't fault the doctor when patients are overweight or smokers and they don't look after themselves.

In March Luke had a big black mole on his chest removed. Luke was tired, but he worked a lot of hours so I just thought it was work. About the middle of April Luke told me that he had a bunch of lumps under his armpit. When I checked them they were just like a bunch of grapes. I knew right away that it was bad news.

His family doctor sent him at once to have them removed. We went in for the results and Luke sat on the examination table and I sat in the chair.

When the doctor came in I asked, "Well, how bad is it?"

She answered, "It's bad. It is really bad." Luke is sitting there and he doesn't even know what she is talking about.

She explained, "It's in Luke's mouth, bones, spleen and everywhere else."

Luke stated, "I will have chemo and that will fix me up."

She regretfully said, "No, I'm sorry but it won't."

Luke repeated, "I think I will have chemo or something that will fix me up." So she just kind of looked at me and didn't say much after that. Up to then he hadn't even been sick, just tired with a loss of appetite. We left there and went to his work, where he told them that he was going on short-term disability because they were going to give him treatments. They hadn't said that, but Luke was in denial. In the end it was the treatments that killed him not the cancer. I called his family and told them that they should come to the hospital because he was in bad shape. Luke died that summer. He didn't suffer and he wasn't in a lot of pain; it was more of a problem with his breathing.

I had a hard time, but I wrote in my journal every day and it helped me. I did a journal for a year after Grant died and then I put it away. Before I started going out with Luke I took the journal out and read it. I couldn't believe how far I had come between that first year and the last six months. I wrote in it every night and if it was a really hard day I would write in it twice. Looking back I couldn't believe the difference in my thought process from when they died. When I reread the journals, I noticed that I had a lot of anger at them because they both could have lived longer if they had looked after themselves.

I used to go to church a lot, but when Luke moved in some of the church members gave me a hard time and I stopped going. I thought; I'm in my sixties and here I'm being judged as if I was some young teenager. I want to start going again because it is good for me and I miss it. God knows what is in everyone's heart and there are a lot of church people that shouldn't be so quick to judge someone else.

I believe that nothing happens by mistake and that everything is destined by God for a reason. Gentle Path and Mental Health were also good for support. I didn't want to use my Pastor because I wanted to talk to a woman that I could relate to and not a man. I'm just more comfortable talking with a woman.

You'll find that men often get married within the first year, but women don't usually move on as fast. If we stay single long enough we get quite comfortable with being on our own. I don't even have to share the remote anymore.

It's like a sisterhood when you make friends that you can go out to the movies or shopping with. Then you don't need a man for companionship because you have your friends and family to do things with.

My friend, Pat, goes on this free online dating service called "Plenty of Fish." She has gone out on all kinds of dates. One time Pat went out of town with some guy that she met online. They called me about a month later to say that they were getting married. The next thing I knew, the guy called me to come and get Pat because he didn't want her anymore. I warned her that one of these days she might get hurt if she isn't more careful.

As far as sexual needs go, you get to an age where you have had enough anyway. But for younger widows it would still be a need that they would be missing. I would like to have a male friend to hold me and comfort me, but not live with me. But you can't find many men that are like that because they are looking for someone to look after them and they don't want to be just friends.

I think the best part of being single is that I don't have to make meals anymore. When I think about getting involved with someone, I think about having to make meals. The other day I had my supper at two-thirty in the afternoon because that was when I was hungry. When you are dating, men are on their best behavior and will do all kinds of things with you. They are great as daters, but if you bring them in don't expect it to stay the same.

Now I spend time and money on myself, like using Mary Kay products that help build my self-esteem and personal value. It's important to work on those areas in your life that make you unhappy, rather than making an excuse for the things in your life that you don't like.

WORDS *of* WISDOM

TRY LIFE ON YOUR OWN

BEFORE YOU GET INTO ANOTHER RELATIONSHIP.

Chapter 8

THINK ABOUT THE GOOD TIMES YOU HAD TOGETHER AND NOT THE HARD TIMES

It's not the events of our lives that shape us,
but our beliefs as to what those events mean.

—ANTHONY ROBBINS

My brother, Tony and his wife came here for Thanksgiving. I was taking them to the airport when Tony told me, "Ann, I don't care what time of day it is, if you need me just call." At that time we were thinking about my husband, Ted being so sick with cancer.

I replied, "I will."

Tony insisted, "You have to promise me and I will be here for you."

I promised, "Tony, I will remember."

Tony left for a convention two days after he arrived back home from our place. My sister in-law got a call that Tony had a heart attack at the convention. I received a call that Tony had fallen and that he was in the hospital and it didn't look good. Tony and Ted were the best of friends and I had to go tell Ted. Afterwards I went down to see my girlfriend, Rita. Tony was heavy and he had a heart attack ten years earlier. He was only fifty years old and he was as large as life to me. Tony died just two months before Christmas and my sister in-law found that first Christmas very hard.

We had a cruise planned for six of us to go the week before our anniversary. It was going to be for our thirty-fifth and my brother's fiftieth birthday. But when Tony died suddenly in October we cancelled our cruise.

Ted never bounced back after Tony died. He had been diagnosed with colorectal cancer and did great for six years. It came back in the lungs, but Ted still had a few fairly good years. Ted's lung cancer wasn't smoker's cancer because it came from the colon cancer. He didn't smoke. Last year when we came back from Tony's funeral we found out that the cancer had spread to Ted's brain, shoulder and bones. They were going to do surgery, but when they went in, it had spread too far. Ted still lived another year, but he was never the same after my brother's funeral. Ted and I were both fifty-five years old when he died. To lose two of them in such a short period, Tony in October and Ted in February, is so hard. It would be a year ago today that we buried my brother.

In December, we knew that Ted wasn't doing very well so we brought the children home for Christmas. Our daughter, Brenda, and son, Sean, were away at that time. Brenda was in the process of moving to a new hospital as she was a Licensed Practical Nurse. In January, not long after they went back to their homes, Ted went into the hospital for a week. When he came home my best friend and I tried to get him upstairs, but he fell down. We had to get someone to help us. Ted was upstairs for two weeks and never came back downstairs. Brenda came home to help take care of him and did most of the nursing. I bathed him morning and night because he didn't want anyone else to do it. I got him his meals, helped him out of bed and looked after the visitors. In the end, Brenda did the medicine with the Extra Mural Nurse. They gave us the best help and I don't know what we would have done without them. My best friend, Rita, stayed up with Brenda the last two nights. Afterwards, Brenda decided to stay at home and go back to university to get her Bachelor of Nursing degree. Brenda was thirty-two and had been on her own for nine years.

We lived in Ted's childhood home and he died in the bedroom that he had as a child. I sold the house within three weeks. It was always my in-laws home and it was too big for me. From the time Ted passed away until I buried him, I had water in the basement three times. It was never my house and we had talked about it being sold once he was gone. We watched this new house being built the summer before he died. Ted wasn't able to make a decision so we didn't do anything about it. After he died I purchased the new house because it had a finished basement for Brenda to stay in. It works for us and we still share our meals. A few times I asked myself why I bought the house, but I did it for her so that she would be comfortable staying at home. We were going to move anyway, as we knew that the big house was not for us. I enjoy gardening and I'm planning a big garden for the spring and I want to get a puppy.

Ted never wanted to preplan his funeral, but just before Christmas we went in and did it. We didn't pay for it at the time, but when the life insurance came in I paid his off. Since then I have preplanned my own burial. Ted picked out his own tombstone. He was cremated, but I'm going to be in a casket.

Ted retired in June after thirty-five years at the Mill. If he was healthy he would have kept working because he loved his job. We planned a retirement party for him. We were going to raise money so that Ted and his two friends from the pulp mill (thirty-five years best friends) could go to a Toronto Maple Leaf game.

He was so excited because he had never seen a live game before. My brother purchased the tickets for them. It was my dream that I could do that for Ted and he had a great time. Ted had his own little room that was covered with Toronto Maple Leaf posters, plates, a clock and cook's apron. Brenda has his Maple Leaf blanket and the new lazy boy chair that he never got to use. She also kept the pajamas and cap that Ted had gotten for Christmas.

The Reverend that married us and the Youth Director from the church conducted the funeral service. The Reverend did a poor job on the service. He started out about when he married us, but then we didn't know what was going to come out of him next. God knows what is in everyone's heart and they don't have to voice it out loud. You had to know Ted to really understand him. He was the most caring man and would do anything for anyone. Ted had a great sense of humor and he fought his cancer like a warrior. People who had cancer said that he lifted their spirit.

We had a dog that my husband loved that had recently died and was cremated. When Ted died we had the dog's ashes buried with him. They were always together and it gave me a sense of peace to have them buried together. Ted was buried on Valentine's Day in February.

I lost my Mom and Dad and I didn't have an interment for them. It was so much easier. All Ted wanted was an Irish wake because we had gone to one at one time. So we decided to have a garage party like an Irish wake. I was exhausted and Rita told me to go lay down for a bit. It was the worse day in February; it was cold with heavy rain and wind. You couldn't go five feet without getting soaked. I had some rest and then Rita came up to get me.

She said, "Ann, you have to get up and see the garage." It was standing room only with some people outside. Ted would have been as proud as could be to see everyone. The party went on until about one o'clock in the morning. They went around the table and did a toast to Ted. Ted was always in a good mood and enjoyed his time with the guys at work. Rita and Brenda put everything together for Ted's wake. I had lots of support from my friends. I worked in an extended care home for retired Nuns and their prayers were everywhere. Anyone would have done anything for me.

Our first Christmas is coming up and I'm in a different home. Every Christmas I have a different theme for the tree. Last year it was in memory of my bother who liked teddy bears. I covered it in Polar bears and some bear light bulbs. A Polar bear was holding a poem for my brother and his picture. I started to collect Toronto Maple Leaf Christmas tree ornaments for this year's tree, in memory of Ted. In October I found a picture frame that said, "Snowflakes and hugs from heaven." It's a little snowman and it holds a picture of Ted standing in the middle of the Toronto Maple Leaf Gardens. The tree will have snowflakes and Toronto Maple Leaf ornaments with a ribbon that says "Go Leafs Go." Brenda is going to work this first Christmas Eve and I will be visiting my in-laws. We have both made the choice to work Christmas Day.

When Tony died I thought, 'Tony, where are you? You were supposed to be here for me.' I needed my brother and it made me angry that he wasn't alive.

When Ted passed away I just said, "I understand." I'm not going to ask any questions because when I originally called Tony to tell him that the cancer was in Ted's lungs, he asked, "Does that mean that Ted is going to die before I am?"

I answered, "Yes, it probably does because you're my younger brother so you can't go anywhere."

Tony said, "There are two people in my life, besides you, that I don't know what I would do if I lost them and that would be my wife and Ted."

I understand why Tony went first; because God knew that he wasn't to be here when Ted died. Tony was so full of life and I wasn't over him when Ted died. I knew ten years ago that sooner or later I would lose Ted if the colon cancer ever came back. But I wasn't prepared for my brother.

In the last five years I have lost my Mom, Dad, brother and husband. You can lose your husband and your brother, but when you lose your mother a different part of you goes. It's been a really hard five years.

I have sleep problems and take medicine for that. I picked up a book called "Grieve" and I read it three times after Tony died and several times before Ted died. I give one to my sister in-law and to a friend at work that had lost her mother to cancer.

After Tony died and before Ted's death I thought, 'God if you want me just take me,' but there is a reason why I'm still here. At the funeral parlor I set up a large photo frame with Ted's pictures on it. I did it the week before his death.

Having a new house and my daughter still at home makes it good for now. I got rid of the big car and got a smaller car. I've been away a couple of times, but I haven't taken any long trips as I've been busy with the house. I always worked so three months after Ted died I went back to work. I took the last year off from the quilt guild I belonged to, but I just started back. I go to a naturopath to keep healthy. My friends and I get together for card nights and bowling, so I have lots to keep me busy.

I went four or five days after Ted's death without eating right. I would get involved in something like my gardening and I would forget about eating and so my meals weren't regular. I'm a big Pepsi drinker and I don't eat right, but that is the way I was even before Ted died. He would get mad at me and tell me to come in from the yard to eat. Ted would make me breakfast and lunch because making my meals was his way of helping out. Ted use to do shift work; twelve-hour shifts, and when he was off he drove me crazy asking me what I wanted for lunch. But now I don't eat lunch and I miss having him ask me. After he's gone you would do anything to have him back, but I would want him back healthy. It's hard to cook three meals and two snacks a day just for me. It's hard because my daughter is working and going to university so she isn't always around a lot at mealtime.

After Ted's first ordeal with cancer we had about six years of almost normal life. Ted went back to work and worked his over time and had fun. We knew it would come back and it did in his lungs, but he went another four years with treatments. The first set of chemo was pretty good and he went into remission a couple of times. From October to February was the worst because the chemo was really knocking him for a loop. This time it was too much for him, he started losing weight and he just wasn't the same.

Ted was tired and was in the hospital for a week. The night Ted came home he declared, "I'm ready to go." He was just so bone tired and weak. He had enough of hospitals and treatments. When I think back, he had some good years, but the last four years were hard.

Three years ago Brenda had a brain tumor at the same time Ted's cancer came back. Brenda was living away then and she was having a lot of headaches and eating a lot of Advil.

I told her, "You're eating too many Advil, just go lay down." You're not thinking brain tumor because she was just twenty-seven. She wasn't feeling well so she went to the hospital where she worked and asked for a CAT scan. She worked in the Neurological department and she knew everyone, including the doctors. They told her that she didn't need a CAT scan, but she insisted and wouldn't leave until they did one. They found the tumor on the back of her head. We got a call that Saturday night and I left for a month with her. Surgery was done and everything was OK.

I had just been diagnosed with a sleep disease and picked up my pills the day before Brenda called us. I took my pills all wrong when I was away from home. When I came back I went to see my doctor because I wasn't feeling any better.

He asked, "How many pills are you taking?"

I answered, "One in the morning and one at night."

He said, "You are supposed to be taking six pills a day." I had read the bottle wrong and when I got out of his office I cried all the way home. I was so stressed that Ted walked the streets with me to settle me down.

Life goes on; you just have to get through it. I always look to my work, looking after the Nuns; it's their time because they have lived a wonderful life. They are ready to go home to God and most of them pass away in their sleep. I find my work very rewarding.

Ted's friends were couple friends when we all got together as a group. Now that I'm not a couple anymore I don't see his friends as much. One of his friend's wife called me for coffee, but I thought, 'We didn't go for coffee before, so why now?" I don't really care for that part, but I know that she is doing it because she cares. But it's like a pity offer because she never called before Ted died.

We were close to a couple that stood up with us at our wedding. I've seen her, but I haven't seen him. He took Ted's death pretty hard. Not being a couple does change things because your not doing couple things anymore with them. You tend to do things with other women. Things do change and I knew that would probably happen. I enjoy being home and having the peace from working on my gardens. I'm not interested in going away or traveling. I enjoy my new house and garden.

I don't think I will ever find anyone that could measure up to Ted or that the people who loved Ted would ever accept. I'm not looking to replace him. Men seem to move on faster because they need to have someone in their lives.

I can do things on my own, but there are times I miss having his help. Besides the loneliness, I am content. I moved in to the new house in April. I can't explain why I needed to move so fast, but I just needed to.

I have a picture of Ted standing by Martello Tower and he is waving goodbye. After he died I had it enlarged to sixteen by twenty and hung it on my bedroom wall. In my bedroom I never turn my light off so I can just roll over and see him waving at me.

In October, I got up one morning and I started crying and Brenda asked me what was wrong. I told her that I dreamt that Ted and I went to Florida last night and it was wonderful. We had one of the best times of our lives and it was comforting, but it was a dream. I had moments where I felt him around me.

I often leave work and pick up takeout lunch. Then I would go to the graveyard to have lunch with Ted. I would eat in the car and then go over to talk to him for a few minutes. Afterwards, I would get in the car and drive back to work.

I gave his clothes and other things away after the funeral so they were gone by the time I moved here. Ted gave some of his stuff away while he was alive and our son took some of his tools. All of Ted's personal items and his school papers are in a memory chest. I keep busy from the time I get up till I go to bed because I don't want to think about it. I don't want to feel the pain, but I have my moments when I just go to my room and cry.

I've had regretful moments and hard times, times when you say "I'm going to divorce you", but that's just married life. Ted was a lover not a fighter and sometimes it was hard to get a rise out of him. We were married thirty-five years and it wasn't always easy, but I don't think about the hard times. I think about all the good times we had. We loved each other and the rest is just stuff that happens in life.

Just a few months after Ted retired he was gone. Sometimes you question, "Why was he cheated out of the best times of his life when we could have really settled in and enjoyed the retirement years?"

Time goes too fast. The older you get the quicker it goes, but I was lucky to have him as many years as I did. We did the first thirty-five years working hard and bringing up the kids and we were supposed to enjoy the next thirty years.

WORDS *of* WISDOM

THINK ABOUT THE GOOD TIMES YOU HAD TOGETHER,

NOT THE HARD TIMES.

Chapter 9

Don't Clutter Your Life With Stuff

*Real courage is moving forward
when the outcome is uncertain.*

—Michael E. Angier

I was first married at the age of eighteen and I had two boys and one girl. It was three and half years after my divorce and I was forty-three when I married Mason. He had three girls from his previous marriage, but most of the children were grown up when we got married.

When I remarried I left my house to my daughter and I moved in with Mason. My youngest boy, Tim, was thirteen and he didn't get along with Mason's youngest daughter. So Tim moved back in with his sister who was in my old house. My other son was married and had his own place.

Mason was about sixty-three when his ill health started. His dentures were old and he thought they were causing a sore in his mouth. Mason was working part time cleaning the Dentist's offices so he got them to check his mouth. They took an x-ray and could see that there was something there. They sent him to see a specialist who told him that it was cancer. Mason had cancer of the sinus and mouth area. He was a very good man who never complained. They operated on him and removed the roof of his mouth. Then they rebuilt his mouth from the skin they took off his leg.

Mason had special teeth made with a big lump that would fit up into the roof of his mouth. It took Mason five and half years before he could chew on anything. I would have to blend up all his food just so that he could have something to eat. Later on he could chew, but it would take him forty-five minutes to eat a hamburger.

Years ago, before Mason's first cancer operation on his mouth, I had gone upstairs and I saw a white figure. It told me not to be afraid that everything was going to be alright, and it was. I had prayer chains all over the world when he was operated on. They had to open his mouth wide and he healed very quickly. Mason never even went black and blue. He healed so fast the staff couldn't believe it.

Mason went to doctors all the time because he had to have all kinds of treatments. They never told him anything and they never talked about how good or bad it was. They just gave him the treatments. Mason got weaker and weaker and just couldn't do anything.

They were always doing check ups, but they never could find out why he was so weak. In the end, they found out that his food wasn't going down to his stomach. The food was all going into his lungs. Mason was able to walk around and even walked into the hospital, but he was always very weak. Mason wasn't a man to complain. Some men, when they are sick, are ugly, but he never was. Just before Mason died they put a tube in his stomach and that's when he gave up. He was just so weak and tired all the time.

Mason went into the hospital for tests because he was weak and they decided to do surgery right away. Everything happened so fast. The last thing he said to me was that he loved me and that I had done everything I could do. I think he knew going into the surgery that his time was coming to an end.

They did the surgery about three days after he was admitted. It was seventeen days from when he went in for tests until he died. At first they thought that he was going to recover so I had an appointment to learn how to clean his tubes. I left the hospital to go home for the night and get some sleep. Mason went into a coma that night, when I wasn't there.

They didn't even take him to Palliative Care because they didn't think he was going to make it. They just put him in a room by himself. Later the doctor told me that Mason was never going to come out of the coma and whatever he said to me was the last thing he would ever say. It wasn't going to be like TV, where they come out of the coma and say how much they love you.

The doctor said that he would never have done the stomach tube if he had known how sick Mason was. Mason was well looked after and had wonderful care, but he never recovered from the surgery and went into a coma days later.

The nurses would say that they knew when I was around because he seemed to pick up. Mason never came out of the hospital. I never stopped to ask the doctor just how sick Mason was. I guess I was avoiding knowing.

When I went into Mason's room, after they bathed him, I could feel something in the room that was different, but I couldn't explain it. His brother, Ernest, came into the room with me and we were sitting at the foot of the bed.

I looked at Ernest and said, "I think Mason's gone." Sure enough he went that quietly.

Ernest said, "Let's not say anything just yet. Let's just stay here for a minute."

I could see a cloud going over Mason's bed. It was the angels coming to get his soul.

I think Mason was tired of being sick and just gave up. He couldn't eat much or go anywhere. He couldn't work or golf or have any life after that first surgery on his mouth. Mason lived about thirteen years after that surgery, but it was a high price he paid for those years because he had no quality to them.

Mason was sick for a long time, but it was still a shock when he died. Before he died Mason asked me not to have autopsies unless I had to, so I didn't. I wish in a way that I had because it may have helped others that are going through the same thing.

We were lucky that we were older when we got married as we did a lot of traveling in the first ten years of our marriage. Mason was seventy-six and I was sixty-six years when he died. We were married twenty-two years and we really had fun those first few years. Mason was my love and I still miss his teasing ways.

I worked for forty-seven years, but I retired at sixty-three so that I could be with Mason. I knew time was precious so I took early retirement and never regretted a day. Mason used to have his lazy boy in one part of the living room and if I went into my special sewing room he would come looking for me. Whenever I was out of his sight for a while, he would want to see me. Mason didn't like to be left alone and hated it even more as the years of sickness advanced on him. The doctors said that he was frightened and that's why he wanted me with him all the time.

If it had been any other man I might not have been able to handle it, but Mason was very easy going. If you asked him how it was going he would always say, "Everything's good" even if it wasn't and therefore he was never an emotional drain on me.

Mason had a great sense of humor and in the hospital he had this monkey putter that he had more fun with. He was always making jokes with everyone. That is what the doctor's thought gave him the extra thirteen years. I can still picture his laughing and smiling face.

Mason's family was there at the hospital when he was sick and they were there to give me emotional support when he died. I also belonged to the Quilt Guild and they were great friends to me. If I get feeling lonely or sorry for myself now, I get in my little car and go out.

Mason had his funeral preplanned before he died, but I didn't do mine until after he died. I asked my son to meet with me at the funeral parlor so he would know what I planned, but he didn't really want to. Afterwards he understood why I wanted to do it and why it's important to arrange things before you get sick. Mason did it before he had gotten sick because he believed in arranging what was going to be done.

Every November eleventh we go up to the cemetery and do the Lord's Prayer and the 21st Psalm because it was his favorite. Mason wanted to get his tombstone before he died, but he never got around to it. I bought the tombstone with his insurance money. I had Mason's regimental number put on the stone because he was very proud of being in WWII. Years later I remembered that he said he liked a stone in the shape of a heart, but it was too late.

Mason's mother purchased a small insurance policy for each of her children when they were young. She also had all the family plots bought years earlier so that everyone could be together. After Mason died I preplanned my funeral, but I didn't pay for it because I have an insurance policy to cover that.

Money was not a major issue when Mason died, but the money had to be watched. I have my company pension and government pension, but Mason had always worked on jobs that didn't have pension plans. All I get is his old age pension. I only get part of it because I have my own pension and they only pay up to the maximum. Even though they said that I would get the widows survivors pension until my death, they failed to tell me that it would get lowered or stopped when I started receiving my own pension.

I want to get into a place where I don't have to worry about house maintenance or mowing the lawn. It's a worry having a house to look after. The children come over to help sometimes, but they are busy and don't always have the time. I can't put up with the worry and maintenance of this house anymore.

I find it expensive to heat the whole house and I don't use most of it anymore. I tend to just stay in the middle level and it's a waste of space. I have lots of family and friends so I don't have the time to get lonesome during the week. But sometimes on Sundays I get lonely because that is more their family time and I don't always see them. I don't like to bother people on Sundays. If I were in an apartment then I could go down to the common area and socialize with the other renters.

I don't go upstairs at all because I fell a few years back and broke by shoulder. My boys moved my washer and drier from downstairs to the main floor and its nice having my living space all on one level.

It's been twelve years and Mason's presence is still in the house. However, I have to sell the house because it's not been kept up and it needs a lot of work that I can't afford to do. I'm on a fixed pension and the extra money just isn't there. This was Mason's house so the lawyer has to see if his children will sign off. I don't think it will be a problem, but if it is then I will still walk away from it because it's too much for me to handle. I'm even at the stage where I won't drive when the weather is bad.

I would like to get an apartment before the house sells and slowly move my stuff over. I don't want any clutter moved over to my new place because I'm looking forward to a clean start. I'm always cleaning and moving stuff so I got some totes to organize my things before I move. I had a big doll collection worth about fifty thousand dollars and I gave it away to my youngest granddaughter. Stuff is just stuff and as I get older it feels like clutter to me. I just want to get rid of the stuff and make my life more clutter free. It was nice to give it to a family member that appreciates the collection like I used to.

The first ten years after Mason was gone I would sew in the kitchen and living room, but I didn't go into my sewing room. I still can't watch 'The Price Is Right' because it was his show and it's too hard to watch it without him. Mason had his routines and everything was done a certain way. I think it helped him to know that he had some things he could still control.

My friend got me into quilting just after Mason died. I found it was a great support and outlet for me. She put my name down to take some quilting lessons with her because we used to do doll making and we sewed doll clothes. After Mason died she would pick me up everyday and take me over to her place. It did me good to socialize with other ladies. My advice is not to spend too much time on your own, feeling sorry for yourself.

Sometimes depression will creep up on you. You have to be aware of the danger of depression. Have friends and get out of the house. Mason and I went to church and spent time with family and that didn't change with Mason's death. We had to give up square dancing and other things years earlier when he got sick, but I still enjoy church and family has always been there for me.

We had a good marriage, but no sex for years. I think when there is no sex that your relationship becomes more of a strong companionship and friendship. Men think that when you can't have sex anymore that it's a big deal. What Mason didn't understand was that it wasn't as big a deal to me as he thought it was. I was happy just having him in my family and sex was just part of it. It just wasn't what defined our marriage. It's different for women because we can go without sex if we have our companionship. I miss the hugs and when he would come over and put his hand on my knee and tell me how much he loved me. He would touch my shoulder and reassure me when I got upset. Even now, years later I still feel his touch and it comforts me.

WORDS *of* WISDOM

DON'T CLUTTER YOUR LIFE WITH STUFF.

TAKE TIME FOR YOUR LOVED ONES

SO THAT THERE WILL BE NO REGRETS.

Chapter 10

DON'T GIVE UP YOUR INDEPENDENCE

No one can make me feel inferior without my consent.
No one can reject me without my consent.

—ELEANOR ROOSEVELT

D anny was thirty-four and I was nineteen when we got married. Dad didn't like Danny at that time so we eloped. I don't think they knew anything about it and once it was done I had to live with my decision. We were married for thirty-nine years.

Danny had high blood pressure for years and then he had other health problems. He was about fifty-eight when he had the first heart attack. Danny was able to retire at that point because he had worked for years. He worked at the Mill for so long that he knew everything about it. After he retired he would go back to work for a while, but would quit when he got mad about something.

I remember his supervisor calling me one day to warn me that Danny was on his way home. Danny had gotten into some liquor and he was mad at someone or something. Danny had a really bad temper and you never knew what would set him off.

When he did have the open-heart surgery, they didn't think he was going to make it, but he did. They told us to be prepared because it might affect him mentally. Afterwards, Danny got really mad at the doctor for something he had said.

I was there and the doctor said, "I told you that this might happen". The doctor had to put a tube down Danny's throat because he was having trouble breathing and Danny came up fists swinging and cursing at the doctor. Danny went for his check up about two months later. I told Danny that he should apologize to the doctor for what he had said and done.

The doctor looked at me and questioned, "You told him?"

I answered, "Yes." The doctor was upset that I told Danny how bad he had acted.

Danny made me promise to write down in a journal everything that happened when he was in the hospital. I did what he wanted because it wasn't worth it not to. After the surgery, Danny began to go downhill. They tested his mental capabilities while he was in the hospital and when he was released he was told he would need to be retested. He refused to go back in and so he was never tested again.

Danny's legs began to swell and large blisters appeared. The doctors made suggestions on how to heal them and I did my best. Danny was forgetful and I told him we had to get his legs looked after. Danny agreed and that's how I got him into the hospital. They put him in for mental assessment, but a few nights later he took off down the stairs so they had to put him into a locked down area.

Danny got violent a few times with the staff because he was confused. There was one, very big, male orderly that Danny fought with because he always thought the bigger they are the harder they fall. One day the orderly said something to Danny and Danny hit him. The orderly fell down to the ground.

I said to him, "I heard that you had a bad day with Danny" and a little old lady had also hit him that day. We laughed it off.

I didn't like to see Danny in the unit because he wasn't allowed to go out for a drive or anything. We knew that if Danny left we would never get him back in. Danny was an outside person who loved to hunt and so it bothered me that he never got outside. I would rather see him gone then continuing to live the life that he was living those last few months.

Danny was under medical care because of his legs and so he was never moved over to a nursing home. Around Christmas time Danny took a bad turn for the worse. His doctor from the hospital was leaving and he told me before he left he didn't think Danny would make the weekend. I think Danny had bowel cancer because he was going downhill so fast. That same doctor called me about a week after he left to ask how Danny was doing. I thought that it was very nice of him to call. Danny was in the hospital and I knew on one level that he was never coming home, but on another level I thought it was possible that he would get better.

When Danny was booked into the hospital in September I was able to get some sleep. Danny would threaten me and sometimes I would wake up in the night and he would be standing over me with a long handled pick. I would just look at him. Nothing happened, but it was frightening.

Two or three times a night he would wake me up to take him for coffee because he couldn't sleep. I would do it to keep the peace. The last five years he lived at home were very difficult for me.

One morning I woke up and Danny was standing over me.

He asked me, "Don't you think you should get up?" It was seven o'clock in the morning.

I asked "What for?"

Danny answered, "You have to go to school." I thought; I don't go to school. So I just laid there and I didn't say anything to him.

Danny questioned me, "What's your father going to say about you being over here?" I thought; Oh boy, how do I handle this one?

So I replied, "I live here."

Danny replied, "Oh I didn't know that."

We would go months without talking because that way I knew I wouldn't get him mad and he wouldn't get violent. The guys from his work would call me up and ask me to talk to Danny because he was driving them all crazy at work. When I got upset with him I would make him Kraft dinner every night for months. It was my way of standing up to him.

Sometimes people would come for a visit and if Danny was mad at them he wouldn't come out of the house to see them. A few months later he would be all over it and everything would be fine. Danny told me that if he knew for sure he was going to die there were some people that he would take out. Thank God he never knew.

Danny had a big Rockwell dog, Rocky, that wouldn't let anyone in the house so I couldn't get Extra Mural in to help me. After Danny went into the hospital the dog started to growl at the cat and then one day he growled at me and I knew I couldn't control him any longer. I never realized how much Danny trained the dogs until Danny wasn't there to control them.

I worried when the dog growled and turned on me that I couldn't trust him around the grandchildren. I had to get my son in-law, Zack, to take Rocky to the vet to be put down.

Every time I would visit Danny he would say, "I want to go home and see Rocky". He loved that dog and I had already put him down. After that I knew I wouldn't be able to handle Danny if I did bring him home.

Danny died a few months later in April. The day Danny died he was going to get up and go out to breakfast so the nurse went to get a face cloth to wash him up. When she got back Danny said he had changed his mind and wanted to lie back down. She turned around to do something and when she turned back he was dead in bed.

The nurse said that she knew the day before that something was going to happen because Danny had been talking to his mother (she was alive but not there). He was angry with his mother and the nurse said that often when they are ready to move on they start talking to someone that only they can see.

I said, "I wish you had told me." I was going in to see him the day before he died and I couldn't get a parking spot. I said to myself that I wasn't walking forever to get to the hospital because I'm tired, so I will just come back tomorrow. Tomorrow never came.

I was with my cousin, Susan, at the coffee shop when I took the call from the Head Nurse. She asked me if I was with someone and sitting down.

I said, "He's dead."

The Head Nurse answered, "Yes. About ten minutes ago." I threw the phone at Susan and I went outside. When I came back in I called our oldest daughter, Tara.

I just came out with it and announced, "Your Father is dead."

Tara said, "Thanks for calling, goodbye." and she hung up. I expected her to fall apart, but she didn't. When I called my other daughter (I thought she was the stronger one) she fell apart on the phone. Danny was seventy-three when he died, but I thought he was going to live for awhile longer. They told me that he had heart failure in October and that he had about a year. But they were wrong; he died in April.

When Danny got sick I went in and preplanned his funeral and then I paid it off the moment he died. It was easier having the funeral preplanned. It still cost thousands and it wasn't anything fancy. The newspaper notice was several hundred dollars at the time, which was a lot of money. Danny was cremated and he wanted buried out at his camp. My son in-law dug the hole at the camp for Danny's ashes and my two daughters and I were the only other people there. I couldn't ask for any better son-in laws; they are both the very best to me.

It's been four years and I don't really feel lonely because at times Danny would go off hunting and fishing and so it doesn't seem much different. Also, I have Tara and her family next door to me. Danny's family keeps in touch and his brother came last year to help me when the water pump wasn't working.

I don't want to go on life support when I get older. I believe if you're going to go then they should let you go, but I haven't done any preplanning. I think the girls know what I want from when we buried their father.

It seemed like all of a sudden, I had no responsibilities. My father and my husband died and I was in control of my life for the first time in a very long time. I got used to being by myself.

The night before Dad's funeral someone broke into his empty house and stole his medals and stuff. I got scared because I was going to move into Dad's house so I got an alarm system. I asked Tara and her husband if they would take over my old place, which was beside my father's house. They lived there awhile before tearing it down and building a new place.

My Dad's house is a very old, large home and it's expensive to heat. The first year I paid monthly and then I went to the power company about budget heating. I can't sell any land because I don't have any road frontage and the land can flood if it's a bad spring. Besides I like having my space and not having close neighbors. There are a lot of repairs needing to be done, but I don't have the money to do it. The old walls are six by six and it was built one hundred and sixty years ago for a stage couch inn. Upstairs isn't insulated and it's cold in the winter. I like living by myself so I don't want to move. My dad had taken the old plaster off the walls and put up gyp rock, but he didn't insulate at the time because he didn't have the money. Luckily for me there was a new roof done before he died. The basement is below water level because it's built so close to the river. It floods every year, which is why it's an unfinished basement.

I thought about selling it, but I'm no good with money and if I spend it all, then what?

Tara wants to fix an area up for me in her house, but I want to stay independent like my father. Dad was half blind, but he lived on his own till he went into the hospital and he was going to be ninety-one years old.

Dad would call and ask, "I'm going to have steak and potatoes for supper do you want some?" No one could cook like Dad and I could never figure out why his steaks tasted so good.

I would answer, "Yeah I'm coming over." Then I figured out he used a lot of pepper and that was why it was so good. It's a nice memory to have today, although I doubt I will ever make steaks like Dad. He never wanted a home care worker, so I would go care for him every day.

About two weeks before Dad died from lung cancer, he said to me "You know you don't have to stay home by yourself, you can come over here with me". I never thought at the time the reason Dad would be saying that was because he wanted me with him.

One Monday he told me, "I've been lying to you."

I asked, "About what?"

He answered, "I haven't eaten anything in a week and now I can't drink."

I said, "You are going to the hospital."

Dad replied, "I want to go to my doctor's office." When I called the office they told me not to bring him there, but to take him to the hospital. That was it, because once he went in he never came back out.

My father died five months before Danny. I always knew that they would go close together. Danny always said that he hoped that he would go before my father. He knew how hard it would be for me and he didn't want to deal with me when it happened. Dad was mentally OK, but physically sick and was still living in his own house. Danny was mentally and physically sick and for years I looked after them both. The houses were close together so I would go back and forth between them. I was really close to my father and he had given Danny and I some land beside him for our home.

At the beginning of our marriage I worked, but Danny said, "What do you need to work for when I make enough money and we have a child now? You're taking a job from someone who might need it so you should just stay home." So I did what he wanted and I kept the house. I had no idea what our financial situation was because Danny did all the banking and told me very little. He was the one that took care of everything and he did a good job. He was thrifty. I never realized how easy money would go. When he was in the hospital I had the car and I would pay off the bills completely instead of the monthly minimum. Whenever Danny would need anything I would charge it.

Danny had a good pension from work and he was getting his old age pension. When he was alive it was well over two thousand a month, but when he died it dropped down to less than a thousand a month, plus I got the widows allowance. It was a big drop. Danny wasn't even going to give me fifty percent of his company pension, but the people at work told him that he had to leave me at least half. He didn't want me to have anything because the less he left me the more he got while he was living. Danny didn't have any personal life insurance, but his old job had a small policy for retirees. Everything I got I had to claim and pay taxes on.

My two daughters always make sure I have food so I'm going to be fine. Just getting the plowing done in the winter can be up to five hundred dollars. I used to work at a golf club and I enjoyed working there because of the social life, but I'm too old now to go back to work. I have arthritis in my knees and I would find it too hard.

If you get married again you don't know what you're going to get. I don't see the reason for another man in my life. I have lots of family and friends around. I'm independent and can come and go like I want. If I don't feel like having supper I can just have toast and there isn't anyone to say otherwise. I can do anything I want and I don't have to think about anyone but myself.

Danny thought long and hard about what he was spending, but I just spend it and worry about it later. I thought I wasn't accountable to anyone so I just didn't think about the money. I wish I had been smarter about it because it disappears pretty quickly. Be careful not to go overboard when you have to manage your money for the first time in your life. Find a family member or professional to advise you.

WORDS *of* WISDOM

DON'T GIVE UP YOUR INDEPENDENCE
AND LEARN TO MANAGE YOUR OWN MONEY.

Chapter 11

TRUST IN THE LORD WITH ALL YOUR HEART

For I know the plans I have for you, declares the Lord,
plans to prosper you and not to harm you,
plans to give you hope and a future.

—JEREMIAH 29:11

I didn't have the full understanding of being a widow until I became a widow. I used to be a pastor's wife and so I helped with the grief counseling, but now I know that I was not in complete understanding of their loss because I still had my husband.

I was about seventeen when we met and we got married three years later. We were married for twenty years and so I was forty and Peter was forty-two when he died of cancer. Someone told me to take one day at a time so that it doesn't seem so big and overwhelming. You can handle one day at a time and sometimes you just have to do it one minute at a time.

Peter couldn't see out of his eye so I drove him to the hospital. I thought he was just having a very bad migraine. He was always a healthy man so I thought that he would just bounce back with some treatments. But Peter was having strokes every few weeks and when they did tests it confirmed that cancer was causing problems in his brain. I was still trying to work and when the doctors came in to see Peter, he either wasn't telling me or wasn't retaining what he heard. The nurse who was caring for him told me that I needed to be there. She recognized the situation and I was very thankful that she spoke up. I was able to go out on medical leave and Peter had medical coverage from his job. He was able to interact with us and talk for about three weeks after the first strokes, but then he had a major one. After that he couldn't speak or move much. Things seemed to happen every three weeks and Peter was gone nine weeks after that first stroke.

You go through the motions at the funeral, but you're not really in it. Most people say that I'm a rock because I don't usually let my emotions show. They don't realize that I'm holding back. That's the hardest part of it; being a widow and yet thinking that I'm not feeling what other widows feel. My pastor was there beside me and helped me to organize things. I can't even remember who came to the funeral parlor. People would come up to me and say that they were there, but I don't remember. When Peter was in the hospital they were always running tests so he had to take off his wedding band. I wish now that I had thought to have it put back on so that he was buried with it. But I didn't think to do it. We had a closed casket because he had lost so much weight. We were in the room when he died and that was enough. It bothers me when people come in just to view the body to see what they look like. We had a stand with lots of pictures on it, but some of the people he worked with seemed upset that the casket was closed. They came in and just left without talking to anyone. I couldn't have stood at the front and listened to people telling me that he looked good. It would have been more than I could have handled.

Our oldest son, Luke, was seventeen and our youngest, Alex, was fifteen when their father died. Luke left a year later for college. Alex is still at home, but works thirty hours a week and has a girlfriend. I'm starting to feel the loneliness more as the evenings are quiet when Alex is out. Luke had a lot of anger at first because he thought that I hadn't done enough to prevent his father's death. Neither one of the boys wanted to visit their father at the hospital when he first got sick. I left for the hospital before they got up for school and I came home late so we didn't really talk about it. They didn't understand how sick their father was until the last three weeks and then they started coming to the hospital with me. They don't talk a whole lot, so it's hard to know what they are thinking.

There is enough life insurance to cover my funeral, but I never talked to the boys about what I want when I die. I had a picture of a couple walking up to a church etched onto the tombstone. The picture shows that we have faith and will see each other again. I put the boys name on the bottom of the stone so that they were acknowledged.

I said to the doctor that if this was a cruel joke then I wish someone would stop it. I'm not at the age when this should be happening. I had no idea how I was going to live life on my own because I had never lived as a single person. I have moments when sad feelings creep up on me. I will be walking in the mall and I see a family with children and I miss that.

I don't hang out with the couples that we use to hang out with because I'm not a couple. It's not just a loss of a husband, but a loss of life style and friends. Other people don't look at you the same way as they used to. I noticed it but I didn't really want to be with people anyway. I was very tired from being at the hospital for those nine weeks. It was taking everything I had to get up and go to work. After work I would just lie on the couch and watch TV, not really seeing what I was watching.

I went back to work three weeks after he died, but I was consistently sick that whole year because I wasn't ready to handle it. I needed a full time job and you can't really get a full time job in retail sales unless you're in management. It is a different lifestyle when living on one pay check and to complicate things I had two sons to bring up. Part of the issue with the store was that they wanted me to come in with a happy face, but how can you smile after you just lost your husband?

A year after my husband died I got laid off from my job. I didn't need another change, but the end result has been good. I was able to take some time off and just go to Bible study groups and hang out with friends. I really needed to regroup and get rested. Then I enrolled in community college and took an accounting and payroll course. I think going back to school was the biggest thing that built up my confidence. I graduated top of my class and they did job placement at the school so I got a good job as a bookkeeper. If it's the right thing it will all go smoothly for you. It helps if you surround yourself with people that are moving forward and improving themselves.

They gave me some information at the funeral parlor on how to pack up my husband's clothes. They suggested keeping one piece in case you wanted to curl up with it. I have never done that, but I did keep one piece. About a month after his death some of the people from the church were at the house and I had a box of his stuff, but it was just sitting under the table.

I couldn't take it out of the house so I asked, "I'm going into the bedroom. Can you take the box out?" It wasn't too bad putting his clothes in the box, but I had to get someone else to take it away.

One day I was cleaning the toilet and I was in tears. It was in the first year and I would break down in tears all the time. My neighbors were a good support when he died. We were not that close before Peter got sick, but then I asked them if they would keep an eye on the house and boys because I was going to be in the hospital a lot. The wife immediately took my hand and prayed with me. They have been keeping an eye on the boys and me ever since.

I took a grief support course at Hospice about a year and a half after his death and it helped me to understand what I was going through. It was seven weeks for one evening a week and it really helped me understand my emotions. They gave suggestions on how to cope with events that would come up; like when it's your anniversary and no one is going to buy you a gift. They taught me not to be upset because you're on your own, but to go out and buy something for yourself or call a friend to do something with. I think Mother's Day was coming up at the end of the course and they said if you want flowers then go get the flowers so that you're not disappointed when there aren't any. I don't rely on anyone to get me what I want. If I want flowers I just go out and get them. There was a widow there that didn't want to move on and it had been years since her husband's death. I looked at her and I knew that I didn't want to be like that.

I'm still having trouble with vehicle repairs and computer work because Peter used to do it. The computer is only two years old and I don't know what's wrong with it, but Peter would have had it working. I wasn't use to driving because he always did the driving as we only had one car. For the first two years I went to full service to get gas and then I had to get someone to show me how to fill it up. My neighbors sometimes ask me out for coffee or ice cream and it's nice to get into the car and have someone else drive again. I have never bought a car by myself and the bank has advised me not to buy a new car. I am trying to fix my twelve year old car and get some more time out of it, but I can't put much gas in the car because the tank leaks. I have to fix the exhaust and the tank so I might not have a choice, except to get another car. I need to keep the payments around two hundred a month and I don't know what I can get for that.

I didn't change the names on the bills right away. I just paid them, but the hydro was in Peter's name and I had to get it changed to my name. It was about five years before I changed all the names. When I had trouble with the Internet I called them, but they wanted to talk to my husband and that was after the name on the invoices had been changed. It can be frustrating dealing with the bills when you're not use to it.

The first Christmas after Peter's death, I had to try to wrap everything when the boys were in school. Peter wasn't around to take them out and give me that time in the evenings or weekends. The church ladies made sure that there were quite a few nice things under the tree for me and that helped a lot. My aunt and uncle would give me cash for Christmas and I would buy myself a gift. I would wrap it up so that I would have something to unwrap Christmas morning. It is a lot of work to get the house decorated for Christmas. Alex does a lot of the decorating even though he is with his girlfriend most of the time. The first time I went out Christmas shopping it was crowded in the mall and I just turned around and came back home. I was used to doing Christmas shopping with my husband and everyone was there with their spouses and I couldn't handle it. I tried to time it when it wasn't so busy and not as many couples were there.

It's hard to make a big meal without Peter because he always helped me in the kitchen. I try to cook a big meal on the weekends and have three day leftovers from it. My blood pressure went up so I had to start eating better and making more meals instead of eating out. The doctor prescribed sleeping pills, but I didn't use them. One thing that helped me to go to sleep was the peace and support I got from reading my Bible.

This year I started going to another church where I'm not known as a widow. I just wanted a change plus I wanted to get a church that was closer to home. The first few years after Peter died I wouldn't miss a Sunday or Bible study. People think that once you get back to work you should just move on. If you have never been single it's a big adjustment to not have a man in your life. Be prepared that the tears and sadness will come up on you suddenly. You just don't know what will set you off because it's just so overwhelming.

I'm starting to be able to be in the house without the TV on. It's taken a while because when Peter first died I had the dog. He was always moving around so it felt like someone was in the house with me. A few years later the dog had to be put to sleep and now I really feel how quiet the house is. When my son came over to see me, I was in tears because I just couldn't handle it. My husband died, I lost my job, the oldest boy goes to college and then the dog dies. There was too much change. I took the dog in to the Vet, but I couldn't stay. I told them that I had watched my husband die and I couldn't watch the dog die. I got the dog settled, but I couldn't stay. They cremated him and sent me a card. It was hard to put him to sleep, but I didn't have the strength to deal with him being sick and I couldn't afford any fancy medicine or treatments on the cancer.

I brought some scripture verses with me that I found helpful. Part of my coping was writing out the verses that helped me. The reason why I agreed to giving my story was so that it could be of help to another widow. Even though it's overwhelming it does become less so as time goes on. When Luke got married on the other side of the country I thought; how am I going to get there by myself, because it's too far for me to drive? Then my friend was good enough to take time off work to go with me and I got through it. I wasn't totally by myself, but the missing link was there. I couldn't have done it on my own. It took me three or four years before I would go away in the summer with the boys. I'm not used to traveling by myself. I did go on a bus trip with a group and I had my first lobster dinner a while back. I'm a stronger person now than I was years ago so I know I can manage on my own.

Peter had given up being a Pastor because it is mentally exhausting to be in charge of a church. Luke has become a Pastor so he took most of his father's library. Pastors can have a hard time controlling a church and it's a seven day and night job. Sometimes when I miss him I remember he wasn't around that much anyway because the church was always demanding his time. My Pastor gets mad at me because I don't call him enough, but I understand the demands on his time from being married to a Pastor. I didn't know there was so much politics in a church until I became a Pastor's wife. I remember when we got a dog and we didn't realize that we needed the church's permission. It happened that the church had Sunday school in our house and one of the teachers was allergic to dogs. When people hear how many churches we went though, they wonder why. But they were small churches and you only stay a few years and you have to move on or have a nervous breakdown. We didn't even own our home because it belonged to the church.

The time came when Peter got burnt out and so we moved back home and we bought our own house. We had lived away for about fifteen years and it was an adjustment to come back to where we had grown up. My biggest fear was if something happened to Peter while he was a Pastor, we wouldn't have a home for the boys. I was always putting money away so that we could buy our own home. The house has a nice front deck on it and when we bought it we said we were going to sit out on it and have our coffee and yet, I have never done it since he died. We had only been here a year when Peter died and sitting on the deck doesn't feel quite right. Now all the savings and struggles I had made to get this house and I don't want it. I would rather be renting because I've come to that point that the house doesn't have the same appeal to me.

At the church I met a lot of widow ladies that don't necessarily want to get married, but want the company of a man. When you get older you don't want to share your space. I asked the Pastor to pray for me and that gave me courage. I had kind of toyed with the idea of doing online dating, but then I thought no. If God has someone for me then he will cross my path. I always hoped that I would get married again, but it was seven years before I went out on my first date. It was scary. He is the postman that delivers to the office and we have been dating off and on. It was hard to start dating again because it wasn't something that I was comfortable with. I don't know how easy it would be to try again if this relationship doesn't work out. The next guy would really have to come a courting before I would venture into it.

Everyone was always saying to me that I would get married again, but now that it may be a possibility, I don't know what I want. When I first became a widow I couldn't figure out how to get used to someone else in my life. Now I'm starting to realize that it might be worth dealing with the change.

One of the things that I had to get used to was that I couldn't read that guy's mind like I could my husband's. You grow up with your first husband so you can tell what they are thinking even from across the room. I don't know this guy and it takes more work on my behalf to understand him. The relationship is scary because there isn't a lot of history. I have been dating for a while now and it is different from the relationship I had with my husband. I try not to compare the two relationships because they are two different people, but I often find myself doing that.

You can't go by how others moved on because different people progress at different paces. In my grief counseling some ladies were stuck in time and never moved on. Some people don't give you time to get used to having a life without your husband.

I can only control my reaction to things and how I feel about what comes my way. You do have some control of how you react, but God has the real control.

WORDS *of* WISDOM

TRUST IN THE LORD WITH ALL YOUR HEART
AND LEAN NOT ON YOUR OWN UNDERSTANDING.

—*Proverbs 3:5-6*

Chapter 12

HELPING OTHERS WILL HELP YOU TO HEAL AND GROW

Change is the law of life.
And those who look only to the past
or present are certain to miss the future.

—JOHN F. KENNEDY

I met my husband at an AA meeting. Vance was new to the meetings, but I had been there for about a year. When I met him I had a three-month-old baby girl, Suzie. I was never married to her father and we split up after she was born. I was in my twenties and going through a lot of stuff. I enjoyed the AA meetings because they were my new friends. Vance was forty-six when we met and we were together almost ten years when he died.

Vance was laid off from work and I wanted to move back home. In order to come back here he had to get a job so he started selling insurance. He had a heart attack when he was out on the road and survived. Vance didn't like his job, was over-weight and really stressed.

To live with Vance was very difficult because he believed that if we looked good, then he looked good too. He had great expectations and very little patience. He expected me to look good and be dressed well.

Things had gone downhill after his heart attack and I wanted out of our marriage. Suzie was nine and very unhappy about our home life. I really needed to get her out of the house. Vance was just livid that I even talked about leaving him. He threatened to take the car because it was in his name. I was working in a group home, but it wasn't steady work. I said that if I have to go on assistance until I get settled then I would and that didn't go over very well. That last Christmas together was just awful because I had agreed to stay and try to work it out once again.

When you're nine year old asks, "Is there any place else I can go to? Is there a place where you work that would take me?" It broke my heart and I knew I just had to do it. I thought; 'Wow, I chose this person to be part of my life and part of my daughter's life. This was my decision and I have to correct it.'

Vance had mental health issues and now physical problems. The doctor gave him medicine after his heart attack and of course he was still on the anti-depressants that he had been on before I even met him. Vance was taking more then he should have and the drugs were making him forgetful. It just seemed to me that he was always taking pills. It was like having two children because you never knew from one day to the next what kind of mood he would be in when he came home from work. I felt that I always had to be between him and Suzie. She was a good kid, but he was always on her because he was a very moody and proud man.

Vance's father died in the war and his mother committed suicide when he was fifteen years old. His mother was on her way to work one morning, got off the bus and jumped off the bridge. Vance had told me that she had slit her wrists and had survived that. She just couldn't handle everything. Because of that, I think he always felt that suicide was an option.

I always said it would have been easier if Vance had just gone with the heart attack because four months later he committed suicide. He went to the doctor for a checkup on Thursday to renew his heart medicine and the next day he killed himself. The doctor didn't know because Vance never said anything to him. If anyone had asked him how he was doing Vance would say, "I'm doing so good I can't stand it." His co-workers had no idea. They called him Mr. Personality because he was so happy and easy going. Vance talked about Suzie and me all the time as if everything was perfect.

After Christmas I had decided that we would separate, but we stayed in the same house for a month while we got our separate apartments and all the arrangements were done. I know now that I shouldn't have stayed for that month, but I had to find us a place to live. Because we were renting the house there was no issue about having to sell anything. That month was very, very difficult. We even discussed visitations with Suzie because as far as she was concerned he was her Dad. It was very hard on her.

I worked shift work and it got so that I wasn't comfortable leaving her with him because when he yelled it would scare her. Suzie would call me at work asking me when I was coming home. It was very stressful because I couldn't have her calling me at work all the time and yet I couldn't be at home. I knew that he could commit suicide, but I just didn't know how or when so I worried about her being with him. He had threatened over the years and when I called his ex-wife to tell her she wasn't surprised. She said that he used to do that with them. Vance was very controlling and it was always you that had to change, not him.

It was a Friday night in January and we had the moving truck booked for Saturday morning. That last month there was some days he would come home and everything was fine and we would pack up things and other days he was very resistant. It was like walking on egg shells. We had pizza for supper and had taken the stereo apart. In the ten years I was with him I had never been physically afraid of him, but as the evening went on Vance got more agitated. The house was all messed up and the phones were packed away because the movers were coming. We had put the mattress on the floor in one room for Suzie and in the other room for us.

By the time we were ready for bed Vance was quite agitated and we had to sleep on the same mattress. We started to argue and he wanted what I wasn't prepared to give so he started yelling and cursing. I knew Suzie could hear all this. One thing leaded to another and he scared me. Vance said some really terrible things to me. He banged his fist against the wall and he had never done that before. He said something negative about my past and that nothing was ever good enough for me. I told him that Suzie didn't need to hear this. He went down to the basement and I got up, dressed and told Suzie to get dressed. We went to stay with my friend, Connie, who was six months pregnant and only lived a few miles away. She knew what he was like and understood that I needed a place to stay.

I had to come back early the next morning because the movers were going to be there at eight o'clock. Suzie asked me if I was nervous and I said, "Yes, a bit." When I drove in the driveway I pulled over to the side so that the movers would be able to get in. Vance's car wasn't there, but my first thought was that it would be like him to go get a coffee and newspaper first thing in the morning.

As we had driven up we noticed a guy who was jogging. Suzie and I got out of the car and we started walking up to the house. My cat, which was a year and a half old, was sitting outside the garage door and I could hear the car going inside the garage. I stopped and Suzie looked at me.

Suzie asked, "Mommy do you think that Daddy tried to kill himself?"

I answered, "I don't know, but go back in the car until I come and get you." If that guy hadn't been jogging down the road I would never have been able to open that garage door. I was terrified, so when the jogger came closer I waved him in. I sked him if he would open the door for me. He went right over and lifted up the oor. The smoke came rolling out because the car was still running.

I asked, "Is there someone in the car?"

He answered, "Yes." I just lost it. I went into the house and I starting running round like a crazy person, but everything was packed, even the phones. The ogger shut the car off and followed me into the house. This poor guy, who had ust been out for his morning jog, got on his phone and called 911. I called he moving company and told them they couldn't come because there had een an accident. That was all that I said and I just hung up. Meanwhile Suzie vas still in my car. The police were there in no time and they drove me to the eighbors. I woke them up and asked them to keep Suzie. I told them that I vould be right back.

I called Connie and she was there in a few minutes. After I called my friend, he called my Dad and stepmother. They came out at once and identified Vance o that I didn't have to. I was told that if I hadn't left the house there would have een three dead bodies instead of one. We would have died in our sleep because ve had been sleeping on the floor and the bedrooms were by the garage. I was n shock, but not surprised because he talked about it many times. Vance had een out there for about eight hours, so he must have done it right after we left. I vonder what would have been the outcome if I had just said yes to him that night nd gave him what he wanted. What would have happened if I didn't leave? But I ave to say honestly that I wouldn't do anything different. I knew that there was lways a chance that he would do something if I left him. I knew that, but I had o take that chance because I had to think about Suzie and myself. So I would still nake the same decisions.

Later, I found a birthday card that he had bought me the week before he lied. Vance never really accepted that I was planning to live on my own. He vould often say that I was the one that was unhappy so I was the one that eeded to change.

You really don't want your marriage to fail so you stay longer then you should I think it was financially comfortable living with him and he was very good with money. When he died I didn't know how to write a check and I was thirty-eight years old. I got seventy-five thousand from the Navy because I was the beneficiary on his retirement life insurance policy. It was nice that the money was there, but I would have managed without it.

As a widow you have to be very selective about whom you discuss your finances with and you need someone to guide you on the right path. The family doesn't need to know all the details about your money. I never knew about finances and you really need some strong advice. I swore that I would never be financially dependent on anyone again and that I would probably never remarry. I was ready to live alone and bring my daughter up. I had matured and I felt that I could do it, but there was some sadness about me.

Before Vance died I went to family services because they were offering this program on wellness and getting your life together. There were four different parts to the program and each one was about six weeks long. I started going to that one night a week. The more I learned about myself, my patterns and why I made the decisions that I had made over the years the stronger I became. Vance really resented me going there. He would ask me questions about it, but I didn't want to share with him. Vance didn't want me to present our lives to others. He thought that I was there to bad mouth him, but I was there to learn about myself. I had just started part three when Vance died and I wanted to get back to it because it was all about writing and understanding your relationships. It was just what I needed at that time. It was perfect timing and I did complete all four parts. I went back to work and I got on with my life. I went to a counselor a couple of times after that, but they thought we were handling it so I stopped going.

Vance never liked any of my girlfriends and they all knew it. He never liked my stepmother because we were close and he resented that I spoke to her about our life. Vance was very controlling because I needed him to manage the money

He didn't want me to have any friends. There were a lot of times I felt trapped and very lonely because he resented everyone.

I believe in the end that he even resented Suzie because he was so tough on her. He would say that I was too easy and he didn't like me spending money on her. He was five years younger than my father, so he was old school that children should be seen and not heard. We had two different parenting styles. I certainly wasn't going to tolerate him disciplining her and he resented that. Vance was loud and one of his favorite sayings was, "God damn it Suzie" and he was always saying it to her. When Vance died I was extremely angry with him, not because of what he had done to me, but because of what he had put Suzie through. She is still carrying around a lot of guilt and mixed up feelings.

This all happened in January and I started to look for a house that summer. I put a bid on a house and it fell through so I had a new three bedroom mini home built. I had stopped playing baseball because Vance didn't like it, but I started again. The coach's brother, Tony, played ball that summer and at the end of ball season there was a dance. Tony asked me to have a dance and we talked. I had just seen him playing ball, but at that dance he had jeans on and I thought that he was nice looking. Tony was divorced and on his own for fourteen years. He asked if he could call me and I said yes. That was thirteen years ago. We dated for a year before we got married, but Suzie felt it was too soon because if she had her way I would never have dated again. At nine years old you don't know what death is really all about. She wanted me to herself and she tolerated Tony, but he is the most patient loving guy you would ever meet. It took her a few years to trust him and to know that he wasn't going anywhere. He never tried to boss her or pretend that he was her father. He gave both her and I lots of space. Now my life is in my own hands and I have a wonderful man to share it with.

Suzie turned into a suicidal teenager with drugs and alcohol. She was very angry with Vance, herself and me. Suzie said before Vance died that she wished it was just her and I, and she felt guilty about saying that. Suzie quit high school a couple of times and then she would go back. She quit in grade twelve for two months and when she went back she worked hard to graduate. Suzie is very moody and has a hard time committing to anything. Every time Suzie was in bad shape I would blame Vance and get very angry again. One time I'm thinking, look at what he is missing and another time I'm thinking he doesn't deserve it. Vance felt that the only way to stop his pain was to end his life. It must have been awful for him, but he did it for his reasons. My leaving may have been the icing on the cake, but he talked about it many times throughout his life before I had ever decided to leave.

I don't think Vance was selfish anymore, because I went to a hope and healing group after his death. About seven years later I realized that I was still carrying a lot of anger and I needed to get rid of it so I took the ten-week course for families of suicide. As a result of that I decided to leave my job and start a suicide program. I did it for a year through the church I was going to. After a year I gave it up, but I will do it again when I retire. I believe that there is a really big need out there. The general public has no idea how many times it happens. I did join the suicide prevention committee and I teach in week nine about how to cope with it after it happens. I think the most important thing to realize is that the grieving process is different than if they died from cancer. With suicide it's hard to understand someone doing it. People either have a hard time talking to you about it or they want to know all the details. Many people are very uncomfortable with it and so they avoid talking about it. They don't want to upset you.

A good place to get help and advice is the hope and healing program through Mental Health. They have programs for grief counseling that will support you. Sometimes you're not ready for it right away and sometimes you are. But you really should get someone to talk to and sometimes it's better with a professional that can be more objective. Everyone in the family is going to have a different take on it. That program was really good for me. I don't think I will ever get over it and it has changed me forever. I chose to get involved by doing the groups and now I lead them. It's like you want to turn the tragedy into something of value. I understand because I have gone through it, so it's something I can give to others.

People don't want to listen to you if you haven't experienced it yourself. For me it was an experience that will always be with me. I have had people say to me they thought I would be over it by now, but everyone gets over it in their own way and what helps me may not help someone else. The first year is the hardest, but it does get less painful. There are different triggers that remind you of the past. In the wintertime when I'm heating the car up it reminds me of that winter day.

I would do some things differently. I could have done better with the insurance money, but I was just in a daze and I wanted to get rid of everything. I gave his clothes away and some of his stuff to his two children. It was like I wanted everything gone. There was a sense of freedom after he died. I didn't have to worry about him or having him call me all the time. Vance would never have left me alone. He would have been stalking me. It would have been awful if Vance was around when I met someone else.

It's a terrible thing to say, but my life really began after Vance's death. It was such a sense of relief and freedom. Suzie said to me one day, "Remember Mom, when you would go shopping and you would hide everything in your trunk until Dad went to work?" She remembers me doing that so I wouldn't have to listen to him nagging at me. I just turned fifty-two and life has been good these last few years.

WORDS of WISDOM

HELP OTHERS AND THAT WILL HELP YOU

TO HEAL AND GROW.

Chapter 13

FIND SOMEONE TO TALK TO ABOUT YOUR HUSBAND

*Things don't go wrong and break your heart so you can
become bitter and give up. They happen to break you down and
build you up, so you can be all that you were intended to be.*

—CHARLIE "TREMENDOUS" JONES

The first time I got married I was only eighteen and my mother was sick with breast cancer. My dad and I never got along; he didn't like me and I didn't like him. I was dating Jamie and when I got pregnant I didn't really want to get married. I didn't know at first that I was going to have twins so I planned to stay single and look after the baby. But when I had twins I knew I had to either get married or give them up for adoption.

I couldn't even come downstairs to eat dinner when I was pregnant. My dad was ashamed of me and I had to be out of sight all the time. We got married and Jamie drank a lot, ran around and was very abusive. My daughters were seven years old when my first son, Tim, was born. Then we had our second son, Dan, shortly after that. We lived locally for about six years and then we moved because Jamie needed to get away from his drinking buddies. The best thing that happened to me was when I moved away with Jamie. We moved to Connecticut and things were good for a while, but then things started to go back to the old ways.

When I was young I never had what my sister and brother had because my Dad was very hard on me. That made me fight to get what I thought was important. Jamie was good when he was sober, but when he was drinking he would beat me up and blacken my eyes. The last time he beat me, Tim said if he beats you again I'm going to kill him. I knew then that I had to leave.

It wasn't like today where you have some place to go. I waited until Jamie went to work and I packed what I needed for the kids. I had a friend who knew someone who had an apartment with furnishing that I could pay weekly for. Jamie kept coming and banging on the door saying that he wouldn't do it again. I think that he had a mental problem because he would beat me up and then he would want sex. We got divorced when the girls were about twelve years old.

I met Cecil through the girl that I was renting from because her husband was a police officer in Connecticut with him. Cecil was divorced and living with his parents at that time. The security is what got me because we didn't have a lot in common. Truthfully I knew his family had money and that I wouldn't have to worry about the next meal for the kids or me. They were teenagers when we got married and it was hard for him to have them around.

After twenty years of service Cecil took early retirement. You burn out quickly on that job and he worked a lot of shifts. Cecil was thirty-nine and he hated the cold weather so we moved to Florida. He worked for ten more years in the

Sheriff's maintenance department. Cecil's dad died and left him a sizeable sum of money. Money wasn't a problem so Cecil could take a lesser paying job and do what he enjoyed. Cecil paid his bills and I paid mine so we had our own accounts. Until the day he died I didn't know how much money he made. Cecil didn't trust anyone and he held back.

I transferred from a hospital in Connecticut to a hospital in Florida. I was a Supervisor for the Emergency department staff and we were a sixty bed trauma center. I got up about four o'clock in the morning and would be at the hospital for the shift change of night to day and then I stayed to see the next nights shift come on. I often would get home about seven or eight at night. I did that for about fifteen years. On Friday nights we always went out to dinner.

Cecil said, "When I come home after dinner I'm going to take a shower and go to bed because I'm really tired."

I said, "OK, I'm tired too." I got up early on Saturday morning and Dan came over to help Cecil build some storage shelves.

I asked, "Cecil, do you want lunch before I go get the groceries?"

Cecil answered, "No, I want to finish these first." So I got in the car and left, but when I came home I could see the police cars and ambulance in the street. I got out of the car and my son came out.

Dan said, "Mom, I have something to tell you."

I asked, "Why are all the police cars outside?"

Dan answered, "Cecil died about fifteen minutes after you left." Cecil told Dan that he was going inside to the bathroom. Dan waited for about ten minutes and Cecil didn't come back out so he went in and hollered for him. There wasn't any answer so Dan went looking for him and Cecil was dead on the bedroom floor. I was fifty-one at that time and we would have been married twenty years that month.

I think the hardest part when Cecil died was that I wasn't there and maybe if I had been I could have done something to save him. The doctor said that it wouldn't have mattered if he was in the hospital, he would still have died. When someone says to you, that it is better they go like that, you want to hit them even though you know it's true.

You leave in one moment and everything is fine and then he's gone. You really can't believe it. But when I looked at pictures afterwards I thought, my God, Cecil looked so tired. You just don't notice it day by day because you're working and tired, so it just creeps up on you. Cecil died when he was only forty-nine. I went back to work the week after Cecil's funeral. The first day I had to come home because it was so hard when people came up to me. I would work long days and eat at the hospital to keep my mind off things.

The estate planning had all been looked after because when Cecil's father died he was very wealthy and the money had been split between Cecil and his sister. So there were trusts and wills done at that time. Investments were in the stock market and his will stated that it was all left to me so the stocks got moved over to my name.

Someone had given me a book called "Suddenly Single" and I never read it for a long time. When I did read it I could see myself in it. I was never angry that Cecil died. We worked too hard and didn't play enough. The year before Cecil died, I knew he was getting burnt out again, so I planned a trip for the two of us and we went away for a week.

Cecil was good to the kids, but he was brought up in a household where everything was black and white. I felt a great relief that I wasn't between the kids and Cecil anymore and for a while afterwards I felt bad about that. Sometimes it was easier to go to work than be at home with them.

I always enjoyed going to church and listening to the music, but Cecil wasn't a religious man. One evening I wanted to go to something and Cecil wanted me to stay home. I thought to myself, if he wasn't here I could go. It wasn't long after that he died and I felt guilty about it. I kept thinking about how I thought that life would be easier if he wasn't here. But who is married and doesn't think that way at times?

Before I met Cecil it was a struggle with my four children so when I got married it was much easier for me. Financially I didn't want to lose that security because I lived in Florida away from family and what would I do on my own? When I was married to my first husband we always rented and I didn't own a home until I married Cecil. We had a nice new home when we got married and when we moved to Florida we had a huge house in a gated community. It was a trap, but I felt I needed that house. I'm older now and I don't think the same way, but back then I was very materialistic.

I had the house to myself except for the dog. I kept the house for three years, but it was very expensive to keep because it was in a secure and gated area with a pool. It was too much house for me to live in and I never used the pool. I sold it and bought a smaller home closer to my oldest son Tim. When I turned fifty-five I decided that I would work only in the winters and would come back home every summer to visit my sister. The first summer I bought a fifth wheel trailer and set it up at my sister's house. It had a little deck and it was perfect for the summers.

I was a widow for about eight years and in the winter I never went anywhere but work. I was lonely and didn't like going out to eat by myself. I called my half sister, Marion, one day and asked her if she wanted to come for a couple of weeks in Florida to visit. I sent her a flight ticket and I was looking forward to her company.

Marion asked, "Where can we go some night because you need to get out?" So we decided to go to a singles place.

I said, "I'm only going for three nights and that's enough." We danced a bit, but she was married and I wasn't sure about it all. It was on Wednesday nights and after the first night I said, that's crazy and I'm not going there again. The music was good, but the men were not worth looking at. The next Wednesday night we went again because I promised we would go three times, but it was the same thing. Marion left on a Monday, but she made me promise to go that last Wednesday night.

I promised, "Yes, I will do it." When Wednesday came I was tired, but I went in and got my coffee. I sat at the table by myself and this guy, Sam, came over.

He asked me to dance and we danced and then sat with each other for a bit. We talked about his wife who had died two years before. Sam had a condo on the beach and I had my house and a boat. He had three girls and they were the same ages as my kids. I had to leave because I had to go to work early the next morning, but Sam said he would call me sometime to go out to dinner. The next day he called and we never looked back.

I met him the first day of March when I was sixty and he was sixty-one. In April we went on our first seven day cruise. We went on three cruises the first year we knew each other. We used to go out every night and walk on the beach.

We stayed at the condo during the week and my house on weekends. Sam was retired, but he was still developing land and selling houses. He had this cough and I kept telling him to go see a doctor. One day in June we were walking and he was having a hard time.

Sam said, "I can't continue because I'm too short of breath." Sam went into the hospital for tests and we found out that he had lung cancer with only six months to live. We decided to get married the first day of March, a year from when we met. A week after we found out he had only six months I was diagnosed with breast cancer. The mammogram showed a lump and I was scared because my mom had died from it. I had part of my breast removed and in the meantime Sam was sick and I was looking after him. I had my whole breast removed in August and my reconstruction started. I got my implant in but it only lasted about six months. After my fifth implant I decided to just leave them out and I gave up on them. I was sick all the time and couldn't keep myself up. Years ago my breast would have meant more to me, but by then I was just tired of being sick and I didn't want to bother with it anymore. I was never sick before I got breast cancer and now I have all kinds of health problems.

We went to Las Vegas for a week in January, but I was too sick and we came back early. Sam was getting worse day by day, but he kept trying to play golf and fish. Sam sold his condo and moved in with me because he was sick. Then we decided to sell the house and buy a small home on the river so we could use the boat without having to load and unload it. The new area was by a very nice golf course with a club house and two pools. Sam lived about a year and a half after we got married. That last summer we went to visit two of his daughters and we visited my sisters, but by the end of August we came back home because he was getting worse. The hospital put him on oxygen when we got home and he lived until November.

Before we got married, Sam had three daughters and his own money and I had my four children and my own money so we did a prenuptial agreement. When we bought the new house we both paid half and it was to be left to the survivor.

Sam called his three girls when he found out he was sick and they all came to the house. I was made power of attorney for his living will for medical purposes. His money and land was split between the three girls. When he was sick I told the three girls they could come anytime and stay with us. This was their time to be with their father and they treated me well. The day he went into the hospital by ambulance he could hardly breathe.

The doctor asked Sam, "Why don't you go on the respirator to help you breath?"

Sam said, "OK" He was still able to make that decision, but his daughters blamed me. They said that I shouldn't have called the ambulance, that I should have let him die at home and that it would only have taken about twenty minutes.

I said, "You might be able to do that, but I couldn't do that." I would feel like I murdered him to watch him struggle for each breath. I had the power of attorney to take him off but I told his girls to decide what they wanted me to do. They wanted him taken off life support so I signed the papers and Sam was taken off, but he lived for another twelve hours.

Sam never talked about being sick so we never planned his funeral. Sam's daughters went through all his stuff and took his coin collection and what they wanted, but they didn't even wait until after the funeral.

They sat by themselves at the service and I told them that their father would be very upset with the way they were acting. When the Minister asked if anyone wanted to say anything they all stood up.

They declared, "We are his real family and he loved our mother." It was so very sad to see them act that way.

I kept our place for about a year, but I had stayed with my daughter for most of that year. I went the first of December and babysat for my daughter for a few months. It gave me something to do and helped me get rebalanced. I decided to stay with her in Nashville and help look after my grandchildren. But I soon found it too hard because I was still sick. I wanted to live by my sister so I bought this old house beside her and I had a contractor totally rebuild it.

There was nothing in Florida for me because the kids were busy and they are spread out all over the States. Sometimes I think that I'm paying more taxes then I should, but I'm thankful I have enough money coming in that I do get taxed. I would advise a new widow to get some financial advice because you have to think about the cost of living. I had two houses in Florida with taxes, upkeep, pool cleaning and it all got too much to worry about. I was very fortunate to sell the properties for a good price.

When I first came back home I volunteered with Hospice and I used to visit with patients in Palliative Care. I taught two classes a month on painting and the classes were about eight to ten people. I provided the brushes and paint, but they had to buy the canvas. They took their painting home when it was done. I always used to mow my own grass and look after my flower gardens, but I think I will get more help next year.

I always went to church. When I lived at home I went to the Wesleyan church. I was brought up Anglican as a child. I didn't really go to church much in Connecticut, but when I moved to Florida I went to a Baptist church. When I moved back home

I started looking for a church that would feel right to me. I really like the Pentecostal church so I will probably start looking at them. I really miss having a home church and I'm going to make an effort to find one that I can call home.

I sometimes think that it would be nice to have someone to go out for a drive and a meal with. It can be very dangerous to travel by yourself unless you stay where there are other tourists. I lived in Florida for twenty some years and I never got to know my neighbors.

I went to grief counseling when Cecil died, but I didn't go when Sam died. I knew that grief counseling wouldn't do me any good for Sam. For Cecil I went to all the classes, but I don't think it really helped because I didn't have the same feelings as the other widows. I felt more guilt than grief over the loss of a loved one when it came to Cecil. I had to work that out on my own instead of being with a group of widows that were sitting around crying and moping.

It was much easier for me with Cecil because it was over before I knew it and also because I didn't have the feelings for Cecil that I had for Sam. When you haven't been married long, like Sam and I, you spend more time together enjoying each other's company.

Anytime that I started to talk about Cecil my friends would change the subject. People just don't want to talk about it and yet that is what you need the most. They don't know how to handle it. Even when Sam was critical, and we were soul mates, I would call my half sister and say I wished it was over with. Then I would feel bad that I would say that, but it was hurtful to see Sam struggle for every breath.

Sam's death was a slow death and each day was one day closer to the end. My half sister understands because her husband was sick before he died. We talked about the guilt we felt because we resented that they took up all our time and were so needy when they were sick. You get worn out from looking after them and then you regret your thoughts after they are gone. They want to be home to die, but it almost kills you looking after them. We all have the guilty feelings we try to handle. Married life isn't easy and it's a lot of work even when you love each other.

WORDS *of* WISDOM

IF YOU'RE A NEW WIDOW FIND SOMEONE
THAT YOU CAN TALK TO ABOUT YOUR HUSBAND.

Chapter 14

DO THE THINGS YOU ALWAYS SAID YOU WANTED TO DO

*You can get anything in life you want if you
will just help enough people get what they want.*

—ZIG ZIGLAR

E motions are different as is the death of your Mother, Spouse or Child. Chris had such a rapport with my Mother and they had so much fun together. The first time I took Chris home for supper my mother told him that if you wear beads, you don't have to wash the dishes. It was a family joke that if my mother got dressed up wearing her jewelry she didn't have to do any work around the house. So Chris took the beads right off Mom and put them on. She just loved that and he got off doing the dishes. Mom and Chris

155

sat there and gossiped and laughed the whole time as we cleaned up the table and dishes.

My mother had breast cancer and she was told they couldn't do any surgery. When Mom was sick I had bought some flowers and balloons for her hospital room. When she passed away my daughter, Rose, took the balloon with a butterfly on it and set it free outside because my mother loved butterflies. She loved flowers, but not cut flowers. There is always some little thing we can do to help keep their memory alive.

My first marriage was bad, but I had my lovely Rose. She had cerebral palsy, but was still very good at looking after herself. She loved people and loved to go to outings. When she was five and six years of age it would be nothing for her to have a birthday party and invite everyone in the neighborhood and they would all turn up. Rose was thirty-eight when she died from a problem with her heart valves. She didn't have any pain and that was always considered a blessing. The church had a lovely luncheon after the service and Rose would have loved it. Rose loved Garth Brooks and so we played his music. The ladies were teary eyed, but the men were crying in the open because Rose had been so loving and full of life.

People would come up to me and say that if they needed someone to talk to Rose was always there. Rose loved to give advice. I remember after the big luncheon everyone was coming over to me, but it felt like it was happening to someone else—it's like you're disconnected and not really there. I think that's a natural defense of the body and mind to protect you from the pain. I don't remember the number of people that were there because I was numb.

When Rose passed away we went out to her favorite restaurant and there was an elderly couple there celebrating a birthday. We paid for their meal because Rose would have loved that. She was always thinking of other people and loved to do things that would surprise and touch them.

I knew Chris because I had bought a house down the road from him. The first time we went on a date he said, "I believe in laying my cards on the table and I'm interested in marriage and if you're not I need to know now."

I just looked at him because I never wanted to get married again. But by that time, we had spent a lot of time walking and talking so I thought maybe I should think about it. Later we decided to get married in March and have a small wedding. It all worked out in the end because of his health. Everything is done for a reason.

Chris was a big hunting and fishing guy and the world stopped for those two things. I didn't go hunting with him because he was a very serious hunter. Chris made me take a hunter's safety course for the time when I might be ready to go into the woods with him. Meanwhile, I'm thinking if I ever go hunting I'm taking a good book with me and finding myself a quiet spot to nest in.

Chris was very afraid of death and he wasn't very spiritual. He called himself an atheist, but I think Chris believed more than he thought he did. He made me promise not to have a funeral, but I kept saying to him there needs to be closure for those who really care about you. I told him I was going to have a celebration of his life and Chris was OK with that. We planned his funeral together when he was still able to be part of the decision making. I don't think he really got the message that there was no hope.

In the end Chris was having so many blood clots that he would just be at home watching TV and he would start bleeding through his nose and mouth. He had a blood disorder called myelodysplastic.

Shortly after we got married, Chris was in the hospital for some tests and a couple of nurses asked me if I had to get married. I was laughing at the nurse's question and yet Chris was trying not to cry because the doctor had given us bad news concerning his health. One of the nurses came into the room and asked Chris if everything was all right.

Chris answered, "It's a hard day with the baby coming and all. What's a person to do?" I started laughing and I could have just slapped him, but it was his way of making fun to ease the tension. Thank goodness that there was no baby because at the age of fifty-three it isn't anything I would want. In fact I would think of jumping off a bridge, but Chris would have jumped first I'm sure. It was amazing that Chris had such a sense of humor.

I don't believe death is final and that is why I had a celebration of life for Chris. We were brought up that we die, but our life goes on. I believe we get recycled and come back in another form. There has to be something to it because there are people that say they have lived before and there is just so much written about it. I believe the people that are in our lives have been in our lives in another time and that is why we are pulled to each other. It's almost like doing a play and once it's over you leave the stage, but then you go on in another form to do a new play. I don't believe in death of the soul. It was a natural part of my upbringing and everyone believed your soul moved on to another state of being.

I believe God is very fair and that we are of God. I think we have a purpose in life and it's like a contract that once it's completed our time is done and we go. I believe you celebrate this life because it's an accomplishment just to go through life, no matter what role your life has taken on. I feel that when life departs that person there is another person on the other side receiving them.

I believe we control everything in our life with the choices we make. If we don't make the right choices either the people will keep crossing your path or someone with the same purpose will come into your life to help you make the correct choices, until you get it right.

I worked in management positions for many years and was used to making decisions. It was really hard to let someone else be part of my decision process. For women that are used to being on their own it's hard to let a man make decisions that affect their lives. Chris very much believed in being the man of the house.

The first year it was certainly a learning experience and there were times when I really bit my tongue. I had to think, "Is this the hill I want to die on?" It really helped me to think first before I spoke my two cents worth. Chris was actually very flexible as long as it didn't interfere with his sleep, food, hunting and fishing. After that he was good with whatever I wanted. I believe men and women need to have their own hobbies. We were together all the time so it was good that he had hobbies that didn't involve me.

You know women, if we get a week to ourselves we think, 'Wow this is great, I can read this book or I can watch this movie that I've always wanted to watch.' When fishing I would sit in the back of the boat and he would troll back and forth in the water. I used to think, 'This is the most useless waste of time and gas money' but he loved it.

The one time I tried to fish I lost it and I never heard the end of it. Meanwhile I thought it would be a lot easier to just go to the supermarket and buy one. I enjoyed being in the boat in the water and camping out, but could care less about the actual fishing. Whenever he went fishing or hunting I enjoyed having the time to myself.

When Chris died I gave his stuff to a buddy of his that was into fishing and hunting as much as Chris was. He wouldn't do anything when hunting or fishing that would destroy the environment or cause any unnecessary harm and his friends were the same. I knew that Chris would like it that I gave his stuff to his friends.

When someone dies you can get very depressed and think of the things you should have done, but there is always something that's not going to get done. If you stop to think about it, you're not finished living until you take that last breath. I made a big effort to not think about what didn't get done, but to think about what we did do and the fun we had doing it. Stay away from the regrets because there will always be something that you can drill on.

Chris had his faults, but I find the thing I miss the most about him was his common sense. I would be on a tear about something and he had a way of asking questions that would bring me to a stop to think about what I really wanted to do. Chris had the most beautiful blue eyes, but when he got annoyed with me they would turn bright blue. I would annoy him on purpose just to get his eyes that clear bright blue. I miss that. Chris was there to lean on and you miss it once it's gone.

Chris had such common sense and he never tried to run my life because he realized I had been alone for so long that it wouldn't work. But he had a way of asking questions and he had this look that said I should be able to figure this out myself. He made me think more deeply about things. I would say to myself, "OK —he's right" even if I didn't want to admit it.

Chris told me what to do with a lot of his stuff. He told me to take his truck and my car and trade them in to get a better car. He had everything listed and what to do with it, but he said do whatever you want with the house (it was his house originally as I had sold mine) but don't stay in it too long by your self. I've been here six years and I'm thinking it's about time to sell it. I did do some work on the house in the last few years so when I sell it, I will not make a lot of money from it, but I'm OK because I have my own money and a pension from work.

I love big cities and could move back to one quite happily. I'm thinking; 'Do I want to sell and buy another house or rent for a year?' I believe when it's time for something to happen it will happen and it seems to work that way for me. I don't mind hard work and I'm thinking of starting my own consulting business about infection control. It will all come together if it's supposed to. I really believe that. I was a wife, mother and wife again so this is my time to be just me. Someone will say to me "Oh, you'll remarry again". What a stupid thing to say to a widow. Until you're a widow you don't really get it. I actually like living on my own so I don't think I will ever get married again. I don't know. I never thought I would marry again when I married Chris.

I know the type of guy I want would have to have a life of his own. I met a guy the other day that said women are very high maintenance and have a lot of baggage. I looked at him and thought, "You're not carry-on luggage yourself." That type of guy would drive me up the wall. I want a guy that will say, "OK, she is high maintenance but she is worth it." Now that's the guy to have. My friends try to set me up and sometimes I get the feeling that as long as he's got a pulse they think I should be happy to have him. I look at them and say, "What is it about this guy that makes you think I would be even attracted to him?" I think I have a right to be adored and I'm not settling for less. Many people say to me, "What are you waiting for, he's single!" I'm not wasting my time, not even to date, unless he is someone that I would want to spend my life with.

I find that many women can't imagine living a life on their own. I say to them that I had many relationships that didn't work out and there is nothing lonelier than living with someone you don't love. If you think living on your own is lonely try living with someone you don't love and don't have any connection with and you just can't wait to be rid of. I remember being with a guy and worrying the first year he would run away, and the next few years hoping that he would get run over, and then finally thinking that I should run away. All through that, there is a loss of self. I never had a thought of being without Chris. We had such respect for each other. That didn't mean we didn't have tough times, but in a relationship you have to work at it.

I would never want to be in a relationship like that first one. I felt when I met Chris that I had found a piece of myself. I thought; 'Now that I've found it I will never settle for less.' The first time I got married because my parents expected me to get married as I was getting older. With the second relationship I lived with him for years, but I wasn't truly in love. When I met Chris I was really in love for the first time in my life. Once you've had that it touches something in your soul and it satisfies a piece of your mind. You think, 'By God it's rough without him, and unless I can have that again I don't want it.' When we bought our wedding rings we engraved on them "Forever Joan" and "Forever Chris".

Chris jokingly said, "Forever? I'm only counting on twenty-five to thirty at best!"

I laughed and said, "So you're stuck with me forever then." He was always coming to me with flowers or teddy bears and how could I ever go without that now? I would be doing myself and the new man a disservice if it just wasn't there.

Chris and I told each other we loved each other a lot and so there were a lot of good memories to help me get through that first year. The memories helped me to heal.

I find the minute you're on your own again it's like you're a threat to certain women. They want to fix you up, but quite frankly some of their husbands I wouldn't have on a bet. Also, my life style can be a threat because I'm free of husband responsibilities and can do anything I want. But life's not the same without someone to share it with.

This lifestyle of living on your own is not for everyone and I wouldn't have done it by choice. But with my mother gone, Chris gone and my daughter gone, opportunities have come up that may not have if they were still with me. If my mother was still alive I would be taking turns with my sisters looking after her. The world centered on my mother and rightly so because she was there for all of us in our needs.

I also had to think of my daughter in every decision I made. Rose was very outgoing, but now that she isn't here you have to say to yourself, "OK, what is it you really want because you can't waste your life." So I thought; 'What are the things I always said that I wanted to do?' I have failed at other things and the world didn't come crashing down. So I picked myself up and looked at what I learned from it.

After Chris died I always used to look for a four leaf clover. I was really bitching one day that Chris had gone off to the other side and was having a grand old time without a care in the world. Meanwhile I'm stuck here doing all this work and you think he would at least send me a four leaf clover. Just then the phone rang, a friend asked me to go to my medical books and look up this certain drug. When I looked it up there on the page was a picture of a four leaf clover. I could not believe it, but things like that have happened to me all my life. I have learned to speak very carefully about what I want.

I don't remember the first three months after Chris died. I really believe its God's way of cushioning everything. Even today there are times when something will happen and the pain is still there. It's not as bad and I've gotten better at letting it wash over me. I couldn't imagine getting to that point when Chris first died. If someone told me in a couple of years time the fog is going to lift and you're going to start wanting to live again, I wouldn't have believed it. In time you start to think about what you can do without feeling guilty that you're here without him.

It's like you have a role in this play and it's written to go a certain way. I can't rewrite the play by second guessing my decisions or questioning why I didn't meet Chris earlier in life and have more time with him. The answer is—that's the way it's supposed to be.

If I need too I can always go back to work and that's a security that's good to have. I really liked the nursing part of my career, more than the management positions. When I retired I was ready to leave that part of my life and move on to other things. The new retirement age is seventy-five because we live longer and healthier. We are not supposed to stop at age sixty-five. My financial advisor tells me I should not retire, but move on to another career.

Going back to work helped me because I could easily have just stayed home and never gone out again. It helped me that I worked in the intensive care unit at the hospital and being a nurse I had to focus on my work.

My first patient when I got back was a man who was officially dead, but they brought him into the unit until they harvested his organs. That kind of helped me because I saw what that man's wife was going through. I thought of it often; about which way would be the best way to die, sudden or with a lingering illness. To this day I don't think there is a right way.

The first phone call I got from someone asking for Chris was really hard. One day I was out mowing the lawn and I had a service man come to the house.

He said, "Your husband should be out mowing that lawn".

I replied, 'If my husband is out mowing the lawn I'm in trouble because he's dead". Of course, you should have seen the look on his face because he felt bad. I have a car dealership that still to this day calls to remind Chris to get service on his vehicle. I keep telling them that Chris died, but they don't put it into the paper work.

When Chris died I remember trying to settle the estate and thinking that I couldn't call Chris on his cell phone and ask him about anything. It really hit me then, when I realized he was gone and I couldn't call him. There is no phone in Heaven. I'm so thankful to my friends and family for helping me get through it all. That support was my lifeline. My friends would use humor to help me heal and that helped me get more balanced.

I took a term position at the University this year and that gave me something new to do. They called me in August and Rose had died in June. I thought that's an opportunity and I'm going to do it. I had eighteen young student Nurses and it turned out to be a wonderful challenge and experience.

I'm coming into contact with people with my new self employment career in Feng shui. There is a great science behind it and doing my own web site and research has helped me. When I took nursing I noticed natural healing was a big part of a patients care. I remembered in the burn unit, if they did touch therapy a patient would heal so much better. A few years later I got more interested in the Feng shui way of life and how the home supports you.

I was thinking about my friend Sheila for about a week and one day I was out walking and there she was. Sheila told me that you were doing a book about widows and she was thinking about me. It just gave me a chill that we should happen to meet with both of us thinking about the other one. I often thought that someone should do a book about widows.

Things come into my life for a purpose. The more open you are to what is—the more everything seems to happen. People come into your life for a purpose, but they don't always come to stay. They come into your life to give you a gift. If you're open to see it at that time you will receive it and if not that opportunity is missed. Sometimes it's not what you want, but you have to take it as a learning experience and trust that you will be able to use it later. It can humble you, but it will make you a better person.

WORDS *of* WISDOM

DO THE THINGS YOU ALWAYS SAID
THAT YOU WANTED TO DO.
YOU HAVE FAILED AT OTHER THINGS
AND THE WORLD DIDN'T COME CRASHING DOWN.
SO PICK YOURSELF UP AND LOOK FOR OPPORTUNITIES
TO COME YOUR WAY.

Chapter 15

TRY TO FIND YOUR OWN BALANCE

I know God will not give me anything I can't
handle. I just wish that He didn't trust me so much.

—MOTHER THERESA

The week before our son, Sam, was diagnosed with cancer he had a real bad ear infection. He had also been complaining about aches in his back. In hindsight these were all signs; but he was only ten years old, so we didn't think much of it. Sam started to lie down as soon as he came home from school. We knew that wasn't normal for him, so we thought he should get some blood work done, maybe the ear infection was causing other problems. Something showed up in the blood work and they wanted him in the hospital for more tests. They did a spinal tap and they couldn't get any liquid, which is an indication of leukemia. The doctor said that Sam needed to go to the children's hospital, because there was a possibility of cancer.

Two days later, on Sunday, we drove Sam to the children's hospital. They did more tests there and it was confirmed to be leukemia. We were there about a week when they started Sam on chemo treatments. Sam was having pains in his stomach and we thought it was caused by the treatments. We brought Sam home and we shouldn't have, but we didn't know that. Sam's bowel was bad. Most of the three weeks we were at home Sam was in the local hospital. The last time he went in they did an x-ray of his bowel and found the infection. We had to get Sam back to the children's hospital for emergency surgery on his bowel because it was ready to burst. They removed the bowel, but they couldn't close him up. They kept him in a drug induced coma the whole time. Sam just couldn't fight the infection because the treatments of chemo had killed the good with the bad. There was an eighty percent cure rate, but when Sam got this infection he wasn't strong enough to fight it.

If I knew then what I know now, I would have waited another week before I brought him home. I think that the children's hospital would have caught that infection and treated it before it got so advanced. They are more in tune than the doctors at the local hospital. No one is to blame and overall the treatments would have worked.

They had to be aggressive with the treatments because Sam's cancer was so advanced. Unfortunately, the aggressive treatments damaged his bowel. Sam was diagnosed in June and died the end of July, within six weeks our boy was gone.

Dad was in the hospital at the time fighting lung cancer and he died Boxing Day of that year. Mom was diagnosed with bowel cancer the following May and died in November. It does bother me that there is so much cancer in the family, but I have no fear of death. I used to be terrified, but once I became a Christian I made peace with it.

Mark and I went to church when we were growing up, but stopped when we got older. When our oldest child was old enough to go to Sunday school I started going back to church. Mark would come once in a while. I got more involved in the church over the years. I recommitted to my faith and thank goodness I did. Even though the Lord took Sam, it brought Mark back to the Lord. It was after Sam's death that Mark started getting involved with the church again and going every Sunday with me. Sam used to ask his father to come to church with us, but Mark rarely did. That really bothered Mark. Mark's faith was stronger than mine once he committed himself. If it hadn't been for our faith I don't even know if our marriage would have survived. Sam's death was hard, very hard and our faith is what got us through it.

Mark was forty-four and I was thirty-nine when he died on the job. Mark worked for the village and was repairing the ball field. He was working on the top of the baseball nets. Mark took a wrong step, fell down and hit the back of his head. He went unconscious in the ambulance. Mark was a deacon at the church and the Sunday before he died, he picked the scripture verse, "The Lord is my Shepherd" to be read. About three o'clock in the morning as we waited in the hospital the pastor's wife started saying that scripture verse, "The Lord is my Shepherd". Later that morning they confirmed that Mark was brain dead and we felt that the Lord took him at three o'clock in the morning when she was reciting the verse. Just out of the blue she started to recite that verse. When I went into his room I could tell the difference. It was just like Mark wasn't there anymore. That was what gave me the peace to say good bye.

The hospital asked if he had signed a donor card. Mark didn't think he could donate because he had jaundice as a child, so he didn't sign a card. When I talked to the nurses they said that jaundice didn't affect anything. The hospital said that the donations would actually save someone's life.

I talked it over with his Mom and sisters. It was my decision, but I didn't want to upset anyone. Mark was a donator for kidneys, lungs and heart. We got letters back from the people who got the kidneys. We had talked about it over the years so I knew Mark was OK with it. My pastor was there because I wanted to be sure that it wasn't going against anything in the Bible and he said it wasn't. So we all went into the intensive care unit and said our goodbyes. I have already signed a donor card for myself and the girls know that I want to donate.

We bought our plots when Sam died, but we hadn't preplanned our funerals. When I purchased Mark's casket I knew the man because he had been there when we got Sam's. He knew what I wanted and he did everything for me. Mark's insurance policy was only five thousand, but it doubled because of the accident to ten thousand. I didn't have to touch that for the funeral so we were OK for money. I was lucky because people donated to the family and I was able to pay the funeral off. Mark knew a lot of people and I remember after the funeral a man called to see if I was going to be home. He came to the house and gave me a couple of hundred dollars. I wasn't working at that time and the donations helped us until the insurance money came through.

I did a new Will after Mark's death, but I need to do the Will again because the girls are all grown up and they can handle my estate. I got the survivor's benefits for the girls and myself. We always lived on a budget and we didn't owe anything on our house. We never had money before and so we were used to living within our means.

Sam died in July, my dad in December, my mom the next year and then Mark passed away. Within three years our daughters, Colleen and Tanya, had lost a brother, two grandparents and their father. I have my faith and that kept me going, but Colleen was fifteen and her teen years were hard for her. There were a lot of screaming matches at that time. I didn't like to fight and I gave in more times then I should have. Colleen would stomp downstairs when she got mad, then ten minutes later she would stomp back upstairs to have that last word. Colleen was very stubborn. She would drive me crazy and so after a bit I would just say go do whatever you want. Colleen would spend a lot of time at her girlfriend's house. Colleen came to me a few months after Mark's death and asked if she could go to counseling.

Mark was strict and he used to tell Colleen he hoped she had a dozen kids just as head strong as she was. I recently told her that it's payback time because she now has children of her own. Colleen laughed and said, "Yeah, I know. The kids won't listen to me, but they will listen to their father."

Tanya never went to counseling, but she is twenty-one and getting better at dealing with her emotions. Tanya had a lot of anger losing her brother and father. She did a lot of back talking and she would argue with me. One of her friend's mothers asked her why she talked so mean to me. Tanya told her that she just didn't want to get close to anyone. Tanya was about five when Sam died and eight when her father died so she is scared and holds back.

After Mark's death I just didn't want to go on. I don't know how to explain it because you love your child with all your heart and it was so hard losing Sam. The love of your husband is different than the love for your child. You're really, really alone after the loss of a husband. When we lost Sam we had the two of us and we could rely on each other. I really depended on Mark a lot; I didn't realize how much. But when he passed away I had to say OK now I'm on my own and I can't depend on him.

I think it was harder in a way with Mark's death because I didn't have him to lean on. With Sam's death we had each other even though at times we felt distressed and angry.

We were married nineteen years and you have all these different personalities living in one house; your husband, the children and yourself, so of course we would have our arguments. But that didn't mean that we didn't love each other, because we did. But when Mark passed away I only had the children and it's a different kind of grief. If it wasn't for the two girls and my faith I would have gotten more depressed and not snapped out of it as soon as I did.

I spent a lot of time with my sister-in-law, Martha, because her daughter was the same age as Tanya. I would just stay at her house and read. It was better than being in my house without Mark. You're more detached from everything going on around you because you're not really with it. There were always so many people at Martha's house that I could be part of the group, but not really talk a lot to anyone.

I never used to have to do anything because Mark was very handy around the house. At first I would call Martha's husband, Jim, to help fix things. After that first year I started to do more of the repairs myself. I also started to make decisions for myself. I didn't realize how much Mark had looked after everything. A lot of it was stupid little things, but they would throw me off balance.

The lady across the road, when her husband died, sold her house right away and regretted it. You can't be sure for at least a year what the right thing to do is. I considered selling, but then I thought that I shouldn't because this is the girl's home and I'm glad I didn't. The memories are hard at first, but now they are comforting.

The first thing I would say to someone is not to make any snap decisions because some of them cannot be undone. You're not thinking clearly even if you think you are.

I was dreading that first Christmas, but we went to stay with family and their house is always full so it was easier. I packed up everything in the car and it was just what we needed because there were so many people around. We went up Christmas Eve day and came back home on Boxing Day. So we got through that whole Christmas by doing something different and not just staying home.

After Mark's death if I laughed I felt guilty, like I shouldn't be happy. That's something I really had to work through. Mark wouldn't have wanted me to feel that way. You feel guilty if you're having a good time and you worry about what other people think.

Maybe it's just me, but I couldn't even think in the early months about another man or going on a date. Everyone is different and has different opinions, but it wasn't for me. For quite a few years I wasn't even interested, but now I think about it sometimes. But it would have to be the right guy and I'm not going out to the bars looking. So I think, OK God, if you want me to meet someone, you're have to pretty well drop them into my life. As time goes on the girls and others will make comments about me finding someone to go out with. The girls will be OK with it now, but they didn't want to share me with anyone in the early days.

Mark died on the job and there was a lot of paperwork to fill out. Worker's Compensation didn't give me any trouble and I got his salary replacement for his lost income until he would have retired. They started throwing all these options out to me and I had to make a choice, but it was all very confusing. They wanted to settle the paperwork so I had to make the decisions within the first few months, but I wasn't really thinking clearly.

Every year I have to send in a form for what I make and the compensation is assessed for the next year. I never have had any problems with them. Workers compensation used to stop if you got remarried, but I think I have it until Mark would have turned sixty-five even if I do remarry. It may get adjusted for the income coming into the house, but I don't know. I will check it out if I ever start dating and it gets serious. It's really important to be careful if I did think about marrying again.

I have a bit more money with the girls being grown up. My two part-time jobs are my social life, plus I need the extra cash to pay for my new car. It's been great because I work most of the year, but I have the summers off.

I used to come home and say I hear this noise in the car and Mark would take care of it. I enjoy having a new car and I did think about a second hand car, but I don't want to worry about repairs. It will be nice to have a few years without any car payments after I get this new car paid for. Years ago I wouldn't have bought a new car, but I now have the confidence that if I lost one of my jobs I could get another one.

At first when I had to put out resumes it was very intimating, but now I could do it without as much worry. I don't fret or panic about money because I know enough to stay out of debt. I do have a Visa line of credit, but I'm very careful about it.

My daughters helped me to blossom by getting me new glasses and an updated haircut. I used to be a wallflower, but I have a lot more confidence in myself now. I still don't like conflicts and will walk away if there are any problems. I used to be very, very shy and I still take a while to talk to anyone new.

There are times when I go somewhere and feel like the odd man out, but they are few and far between. I don't like to walk into a place by myself even if I know everyone. So I will ask if anyone else is going that I can pick up or go with. You have to make the effort to phone them because they don't understand how you're feeling. I would go anyway, but I feel more comfortable walking in with someone.

Women get together as a group to travel because if we didn't we wouldn't get to go. If you don't have a husband to travel with then you can go with groups. Women have fun together so you have to let everyone know that you're willing to travel. I'm hoping to go on a cruise with three other women next winter. Two of the women are my sister in-laws. I told them the next time that they go anywhere I'm going because I want to get away and do some traveling.

I was doing some sewing and quilting with my friend, Patty. I just started working, about a month before Mark died, at her sewing store. I worked on and off for free sewing and quilting supplies. I got into tole painting after Mark died. Martha and I started taking lessons once a week. I continued with the lessons and that was my sanity. It gave me something that wasn't expensive to do in the evenings. I could take out my paints and time would fly by. I watch TV, but I don't want to get caught up with TV being my only company. I continue to tole paint and I look forward to taking a class on painting animals.

I don't usually have a problem with sleeping because I keep the TV on for the noise. I don't like it when it is too quiet in the house. I often fall asleep on the couch watching the TV late at night. Once I'm asleep I don't wake up till the morning. Some nights I do have a hard time and I will lie there watching the clock. I don't want to take anything so I just get through it.

At first I didn't like being alone, but I had the girls here. How it's kind of weird at times, but I have the dog for company and that helps. The dog lets me know if someone is around the house.

My first advice is not to make any snap decisions. To take one day at a time because there are going to be good days and there are going to be bad days. Days when you feel like you're not going to make it through. And sometimes it's one hour at a time that you have to get through. It does get easier and that is the hardest thing to believe at the beginning, but it is true.

I wonder how people who don't have faith can get through it. I know that Sam and Mark are in heaven and I know that I will see them again. I have that, but if you don't have that belief I don't know how you can do it. I think that may be why it's harder on some women. If they don't have that faith then maybe they should have some counseling and try to find their peace.

Although I did have my missing times I never got into a depressed state. I had a great support system with my church and my family. If you're having bad days go out of the house. If you don't have a vehicle, then go for a walk. Don't stay in the house, get out. Do something, don't just sit there. If you're depressed it will only build, build and build until it gets to a point when you don't want to do anything or socialize with anyone. It can be a trap so be aware and avoid it. Develop some social life like going to bowling, library, and volunteer groups. There are lots of things you can do; you just have to force yourself to get out of your comfort area.

It's been said to me that I would make a good grief counselor because I have lost a child and my husband. As a counselor I can have empathy with their grief. They need to talk to someone who has been there. I may actually look into that some day because it would also be good for me.

I went to a church weekend retreat after Mark died and they had all kinds of speakers. One of the speakers was a widow talking about life after and it helped to hear her. She knew and understood because she had gone through it herself. How can someone else tell me when they haven't experienced it themselves?

It's been fifteen years and now I think I'm too independent for another man in my life. I come and go as I want. If I want to go away for the weekend I just put the dog in the kennel and go. I don't have to answer to anyone because the girls are grown up and living out on their own. At work, it is all girls and we joke around about me getting married again. I joked back that the guy has to be a carpenter, electrician and cook, with lots of money. I joke, but it's partly true because I want more if I marry again. I don't want anyone that's dependent on me. He would have to have his own life.

The girls at work are friends that I can have fun with. Someone just said to us that we must be sisters because of the way we tease and joke amongst ourselves. Women do need other women because those friendships help us to have confidence. Women need each other to laugh with. I know I can call my friends or sister in-laws anytime. I don't have to be alone because I have them in my life.

There are still times that I think, how am I going to get through this day. They are not as often, but there are still days when something goes wrong and I say, "Why am I here alone trying to deal with this?

Everyone has their own way of handling their grief. Nothing is set in stone of how you have to deal with it. What works for me may not work for another widow. That's the balance a widow has to find, it's her journey.

With Mark I went through anger saying, "Why did you step on that net? How could you be so stupid? You know better? Why did you leave me?"

I went through my bits of anger and sadness. You really don't know what's going to come out at times. You can be mad, you can be happy, you can be sad; it's just part of the grieving process.

Where it might take one person two months, it might take the next person two years before they are back on their feet again. Don't feel bad if it's been two years and you're still not ready to focus on everything. You may not be ready to jump right back into everything. Everyone has their own time limit.

WORDS *of* WISDOM

A WIDOW HAS TO FIND HER OWN BALANCE.
IT'S YOUR JOURNEY AND YOU HAVE TO HEAL
AT YOUR OWN PACE.

Chapter 16

THE AUTHOR'S STORY

I expect to pass through this world but once.
Any good things, therefore, that I can do,
any kindness that I can show a fellow being,
let me do it now. Let me not defer or neglect it.

—STEPHEN GRELLET, *1773–1855 Quaker Missionary*

When we were dating I would call Donnie, "Charlie Brown" and he would call me "Snoopy". Throughout our twenty-seven years of marriage, in good times and bad, we always signed our cards with those nick names.

I remember when we spent our twenty-fifth wedding anniversary at the cottage. Donnie went down earlier that day and I came later because I had to work. When I turned into our road I saw this huge sign nailed to the telephone pole. On it he had sprayed in red paint "Happy 25th Anniversary Snoopy, I love you." Donnie was romantic from our very first date so I didn't think anything of it. It was normal to me, but now I realize how special and rare it was to have such a romantic husband.

My parents divorced when I was four and Mom brought us up; all five sisters! I had never seen a man shave until I got married. I think I had this picture in my mind of a perfect marriage and I didn't realize that couples do argue and that marriage can be difficult. I was hard on Donnie and when he was alive I blamed all of our problems on him, but now I realize that it was both of us.

Donnie started drinking when his father died and he had to go to the morgue to identify the body. Donnie was soft hearted and he never got over seeing his father like that. He couldn't shake that picture from his mind and it always bothered him. I wish I had him back so I could tell him how much I appreciate how he loved me, his romantic ways and how hard he worked to provide for his family.

We were on vacation at the cottage when Donnie passed out while talking on the phone. He went for some tests and two weeks later we found out he was full of cancer, in the lungs, liver and lymph nodes. In the hospital when they told Donnie that they were not going to operate I knew that it was terminal. Donnie was sitting on the side of his hospital bed and I was in one chair and Dr. Scott was in the other chair. The very first thing that Donnie said was that he was going to fight it. I went and sat by Donnie and told him that if that was what he wanted then that is what we would do.

While Donnie was in for tests, Dr. Scott came everyday while on his rounds. Donnie had so much trust in Dr. Scott and seeing him helped to keep Donnie calm. Dr. Scott tried for years to get Donnie to look after himself, but what can you do if the person doesn't want to follow your advice?

Donnie lived a normal life up until the time he first passed out. If they found out a year earlier would it have saved him or would he have spent the last year of his life in treatments and in pain? We will never know. A week after we found out, Donnie died sitting at the kitchen table without having been in any pain or having any treatments. I was in shock and angry on the phone with Dr. Scott.

I said, "Donnie did it to himself, he wouldn't quit smoking." Dr. Scott was on the phone trying to reason with me. He said, "Now Mary, don't blame Donnie. It's not like he did it on purpose." I remember thinking that I didn't want to be reasoned with. What did Donnie think was going to happen? The doctor released me from this anger by saying that it just happens—everyone dies and it's not avoidable. Dr. Scott asked me if I wanted to have an autopsy done.

In grief I said, "Donnie's dead. What good would an autopsy do? I don't care what killed him, he's gone." He died fast and painlessly and after talking to other widows that have had husbands die long painful deaths, I realized that it was a blessing the way Donnie died. My regret is that I didn't tell him how much I loved him because I thought I had time.

That last week we didn't talk about the cancer or what the future may hold. We avoided talking about it because we were not ready to face the possibility of his death.

Dr. Scott told me that Donnie probably had a blood clot that got to his lung. As time went on I realized that he didn't want to die. Donnie didn't understand how his life choices were affecting his health. I felt he should have looked after himself better and then I wouldn't be without him. Then I felt guilty that I was angry with Donnie and I felt that no other widow would be as angry with their husband as I was.

We were too busy and I didn't take the time with Donnie that I should have. That is a regret I have, that I didn't slow down and try to understand what was going on with Donnie and his drinking. Donnie was an alcoholic and we had some hard times. I struggled when writing the word "alcoholic" because it is a harsh word. It's hard to bare our troubles for the world to see, but I owe honesty to the widows who have shared their stories. But who can be married for twenty-seven years and not have their share of problems? That is life and it in no way takes away from our love.

I will never give up my memories because I enjoyed being married. I didn't have the stress of being single and being alone. I was angry that it didn't turn out as Donnie and I had planned. We should have been able to enjoy our later years together because we had both worked so hard to get our home, cottage and the children educated. This was supposed to be our time. It's not right or wrong it's just what I felt. For me when I'm with women that still have their husbands and they are complaining, I'm thinking don't do that because that is what I used to do and I regret it now.

Our daughter, Angela was just finishing her Licensed Practical Nurse (LPN) degree when Donnie died. Tuesday morning Donnie died while sitting at the kitchen table and Angela tried to revive him and couldn't. It was very traumatic for her and months later she still had a hard time coming into the dining area where he died. Donnie died and she had to write her Nurses certification papers the next day. They would not reschedule and if she didn't write them she would have to wait for another six months because they are only written twice a year. Angela had just finished the program and studied for it so she had to do it. We were all worried that she would be too stressed, but I think that she was still in shock and that's why she was able to do it.

I was running around the morning Donnie died like a crazy woman because his funeral wasn't preplanned. It was so hard arranging everything in one day that afterwards I preplanned mine. I would recommend to anyone that preplanning is a gift to the family left behind. I did it so that the children won't have that responsibility when I die.

When you're at the funeral it's like you are socializing as you talk to everyone. But you are not there because you're still in a daze. You're walking and talking, but you're disconnected from it. Months later you wonder who was there because you don't remember. Now I take the time to sign the book when I go to a funeral home because I know that they won't remember. I don't know what I would have done without the support of my Uncle Wayne, Aunt Sheila and my four sisters. Donnie's best friend, Bobby stayed at the funeral parlor every minute. He had worked for years with Donnie and he took care of all the men that came in to pay their respects. The men from Donnie's work came to the funeral and told stories about Donnie and his practical jokes. It was good for the children to hear that their father was a good friend and a hard worker.

Our son, Nathan had bought Donnie a watch for Christmas, which he always wore. When Donnie was laid out he was wearing the watch and I thought that I should have it for Nathan to keep. I asked the funeral parlor if they would get it for me, but what I didn't know was that it would leave an imprint on Donnie's skin because they had already prepared him. Nathan noticed the imprint where the watch had been and so it didn't turn out to be a good keepsake.

I took my time doing our tombstone. I had our wedding picture and date put on the stone. Donnie always struggled with his drinking so I put the AA serenity prayer on the back of the stone. On the front of the stone the bottom line reads, "Charlie Brown and Snoopy Forever". I wanted the tombstone to be personal and for it to tell about our lives together.

Donnie didn't go to church on a regular basis, but he did believe in God and was a good man. I thought I should have made him go to church more and that I was responsible for not ensuring that he knew God better. You just take on so much more guilt than you have to. But that's not true because it was Donnie's relationship with God, not mine. I had asked Donnie when we first found out about the cancer if he wanted to talk to a minister.

He said, "Oh no, we will have lots of time." In the end there was no time so I guess it's true what they say about not putting things off because only God knows how much time you have.

The original Will is like gold because a copied Will is worthless unless it is notarized by the lawyer. Get notarized copies to give to those that want one and keep the original. I made a new Will, preplanned and paid for my funeral and got all my paperwork together in one place for the children. I even went out and got a small safety deposit box for home to keep everything in. I've also learned to organize my business papers so that when I die the children will be able to find everything they need to settle the estate. Funny thing, after Donnie died I found keys all over the place, but I had no idea what half of them belonged to. I identified each known key with a colored label and I wrote on the label what the key was for.

Angela works the night shifts and I work days. When I want to go over any pictures or memories I do it when Angela is at work so that she doesn't see me upset. I don't want her to feel my pain along with her own. I cleaned out Donnie's clothes and personal things one night when I was home alone. I cried all the way through it, but it was one of those things that had to be done so I just did it. I kept some things I wanted and put them in a tote that fits under the bed. I gave both Angela and Nathan a keepsake box of stuff from their Dad.

The second week after Donnie's death, Angela bought me a huge, oversized stuffed cat to sleep with. I would cuddle up with it and the bed didn't seem so empty. I slept with it for six months and then I gave it away. The bed is unbalanced, there were two and now there is only one. I bought a new house after he died, but when I moved in I was disappointed because it didn't give me the peace that I thought it would. I still miss Donnie and it's still an empty bed and moving didn't change or help that lost feeling.

I had a problem with Donnie's special sport package that he had with our cable company. It was expensive and when I tried to cancel it they gave me a lot of trouble. Every month the bill would come in with the charge on it and I would have to call them. On the third month I called them and I started to cry on the phone. I just didn't want to go over it again. I hated having to say that my husband was dead. Husband and dead together in a sentence was so foreign to me that I just couldn't seem to get it out. Angela took the phone from me and she asked to speak to a supervisor. The supervisor said that if I sent them Donnie's death certificate they would be able to stop the sports package and credit the account. I don't know what I would have done if Angela hadn't been home to get it settled.

First Christmas; I didn't want that Christmas. Angela had gotten Christmas Eve and Christmas day off work because she was worried about me. I had three Christmas dinners that year. I went to my Uncle Wayne's and Aunt Sheila's for Christmas Eve supper. Then Angela and I went to Nathan's and his wife, Andrea's for Christmas supper. On Boxing Day we went to see Donnie's mother, Shirley for another Christmas supper. I thought that I can't pretend that it's a normal Christmas so I just did things different then we usually did.

In the spring when Bobby and his brother Jimmy helped me open up the cottage there was all Donnie's stuff. His jacket hanging as he left it and his spare glasses on the counter. It was as if I had stepped back in time to when we had just been at the cottage together. It was terrible. I took his jacket and held it to my face so that I could breathe in his smell. I had never felt as lonely as I did that day.

I had thought of selling the cottage because it was really hard going there that first summer without Donnie. We had such good times there because when we were together we would go visiting or stay in by the fireplace and play cribbage or cards. We both worked hard so the cottage was our quiet time together.

Donnie had so proudly bought a John Deer lawn mower four months before he died. He just loved mowing the lawn at the cottage. No one used it but Donnie and the first time I had to start it up and mow the lawn I was miserable. It was just so wrong that it wasn't Donnie on his tractor but me. I used to go shopping with my Aunt Sheila and when I got back Donnie would have all the lawn mowed and the place would look like a million dollars, but now it's up to me to do all the yard work. I loved going down to the cottage a day before Donnie and having a quiet evening to myself, but now I'm always there by myself and I wish he was with me. It's true that you don't appreciate what you have until it's gone.

I had a dream where I heard Donnie's voice and I woke up and wrote his words down because I didn't want to forget them.

Donnie said, "It's going to be OK Mary" and that is all he said, but it was so clear and I heard it just like he was laying there beside me. I had mixed feelings because it gave me a sense of peace, but also a sense of sadness because I liked hearing Donnie's voice.

Sometimes we think that if we get professional help we are admitting that we can't handle it. But I think that it's important that we don't try to pretend that everything is alright. If we need to talk to someone then we should do it. It takes a strong woman to know when to go for help and not hide her feelings. If you think you're handling it, you don't think you need help. And if you don't think you need help you won't go get it. That is the danger of not acknowledging your feelings. Women who still have their husbands try to help, but they don't really understand because they don't have that empty spot in their lives.

One day I was driving home from work and I just had this wave of homesickness for Donnie. I just missed him. I had this sense of loneliness and I don't know what caused it, but it just swept over me and I started to cry. It's like when you're away at summer camp and missing home. It's been a while since I felt that loss of love and Donnie's smile, but it comes up on me at the oddest times.

When Donnie died he was fifty-three and because he was under the fifty-five pensionable age I had this window where I could take all his pension money out of the fund and control it myself. I'm thinking; 'I have to make a decision, what should I do? Which is the best way?' If I leave it there I get a check every month starting at once until I die and I'm only fifty years old. But when I die that's the end of it and the children don't see any of it. I had to make the decision within the first few months and so I drew it all out and invested it. This way the children will get what's left when I die. Also, it will continue to grow with the interest it earns until I start to draw it out. I still find it confusing as to the best way, but I think in the long run that it's better that I have control of the lump sum from Donnie's pension. My insurance agent, Todd Soper from Sun Life Financial is a great advisor to me. I don't know what I would have done with the insurance and pension without Todd's advice.

As a widow you have to get financial advice and family may not know the best way to handle money. Family may want to help, but unless they are trained in finances they may do more harm than good.

When Donnie died I realized that he did much more than just work, he kept me balanced. I was more emotional and he was more relaxed so I could go to him when I needed to be comforted. Donnie evened me out and I wasn't grounded after he died. I still feel like I'm floating and I don't feel settled. You think you're OK, but everything is so off centered when your husband dies.

I do programming at the hospital and the first time I went there I was in the area where Donnie had some tests done. I'm doing my rounds and I'm standing outside his room and I'm thinking just a few weeks ago I was standing here with Donnie.

When Donnie was having his ultrasound done I was talking to the girl that I had trained on the ordering system. When I was back in that area she came up to me and asked how Donnie was doing. Of course she didn't know. I started crying and I said, "He didn't make it." She took me into a private room and I kept saying, "I'm so sorry" because I couldn't stop crying. I wasn't prepared for seeing her and dealing with the fact that the last time I had seen her I had Donnie with me.

I thought that I was handling it, but I wasn't ready to talk about it or actually say that Donnie was gone. I finished that day out, but didn't go back for another two weeks. I went home and cried my eyes out and thought to myself; 'What are you doing back so soon?'

There were days when I was so weary that I would just want to crawl into bed and cuddle up in my blankets, forgetting about the outside world. I don't think there is anything wrong with that. Sometimes I just needed to ride it out, after all so many changes in so short a time were bound to wear me down.

I went out to my brother in-law's birthday with my sisters and their husbands. It was the first time out with them as a group and it was very odd to me. Even though I was with them I felt that I was by myself. It got easier as time went on, but I'm still an odd person when we get together. There were always five sisters and our husbands, but now there are nine instead of ten.

I make a lot of soups and stews in the slow cooker and freeze it in single portions because I don't like to cook for one person. It just doesn't seem worth the work. Donnie was a meat and potato guy, but when I cooked like I used to I was throwing out more then I was using. There was a really big change in my eating habits in the first year and I gained some weight. I would go through the pickup window at the different fast food places and my diet was just terrible. Out of boredom in the evenings I would go back and forth to the fridge. I wasn't eating well, my face broke out and I was just plain tired. I never got a full night's sleep, but I was also going through menopause and that didn't help my moods or sleep. I joined a woman's gym and starting exercising to get rid of some stress. It helped me to sleep better and it felt good doing something positive.

I put my feelings on hold and I tried not to cry that first few months. I kept it back because I was afraid to really feel for fear that it would hurt and I wouldn't be able to control it. I'm faced with many tough questions. Who am I? Where am I going in life? What do I want? What are my goals and plans to achieve these goals?

I have to fight down the fear of inability and self-talk myself into positive action. Small steps, taken with confidence, have helped me move forward. I found that whenever I reached out to help someone else, I ended up feeling better. It gave me some self-worth and made me appreciate what good things I still had going for me.

Little by little I realized that I didn't have to cater to other people's needs all the time. I started to slowly change as circumstances forced me into a new lifestyle. I questioned my habits and the necessity of continuing in the way I cooked, shopped, etc. It changed because as a widow I no longer had to do anything at anyone's timetable but my own. I started taking control, making decisions and trying new things.

Not having my husband changed how I spent my time, especially the times I used to spend just with him. Things are different now and I find that I'm often the odd woman out, no longer part of a couple. When friends invite me anywhere, I quickly say yes. Sometimes it's a disappointment, but mostly it's a good time and I meet some new people. I just tell everyone that if they are going somewhere to ask me because I'm willing to go anytime. I don't want to stay home and miss any chances to travel. This is where meeting other women and getting involved in groups like "The Red Hat" society has been good for me. There is nothing like going out with other women and just having fun. It is healing for my soul when I laugh and enjoy myself.

I stretch myself because I'm afraid of growing old and having regrets for people and places I never made the effort to explore. A new social life awaits me in travel, hobbies and perhaps later new relationships. My view of life has changed and people are more important, while things have lost their appeal.

I didn't know anything about curling and didn't even watch it on TV. My friend, Monique, told me about Carleton Curling Club, Ladies Business League. The first year I went every Monday night. No one knew me besides Monique, so I could hide from being a new widow. I joined a month after Donnie's death and I wasn't really into it. In fact I was pretty much a dead pan that first year, but I went because it forced me to socialize. The second year I started curling on weekends and social events. I started to have fun and join in more with everyone. Curling was just what I needed to get out of my comfort zone and meet new people. It's important to socialize with women friends by joining different things like bowling, curling, darts, cribbage, Red Hat groups and volunteering.

The first year anniversary I had Donnie's family and Bobby at the house for a small get together and luncheon. It was something I wanted to do in Donnie's memory, but I wouldn't do it every year. At first I didn't want to talk about Donnie's death, but after a while I realized that it made me feel better. I started to recall funny things he did and how good he was to older people that others avoided. In some ways I wanted that first year to be behind me. I hated that first Christmas, first birthday and first anniversary. On the other hand that first year family and friends are there with more support. They rally around with kindness and it's less lonely.

I went up to the grave site the second year and I felt sorry for myself because no one called me and I was there alone when the first year everyone was there for me. They thought I must be getting better and they moved on with their lives, taking some of their support with them. When I got home I thought there would be some messages on the phone, but there wasn't. How strange that I didn't want to talk to anyone, but when no one called I felt dumped, that no one remembered or cared. This is how a widow is, struggling to find that balance. But in fairness I didn't put out the vibes that I needed anyone.

That's when I realized that I'm responsible for myself. Everyone has moved on because Donnie's death didn't change their lives like it did mine. Now that I'm on my second year, I look back on that first year and think about how I made decisions about buying a house and investments when I wasn't really myself. I was an empty shell that was just getting by. Even in the second year I'm still getting my feet under me. I'm still struggling and although in many ways it has gotten better, other times I feel myself slipping into unhappiness and not knowing how to save myself.

Lately everyone seems to be trying to match me up with someone for "companionship." Someone recently asked me when I was going to take my wedding band off. That threw me because it had never crossed my mind. I guess I still feel married and it's Donnie that I'm missing. People would say that I need a man, but that's not true. I need love and companionship and at this time I'm getting that from family and friends. I always knew that Donnie loved me so I don't want to settle for less than that. I would have to be in love again and it would have to be the right man at the right time in my life.

I have made room for friends in my life. In fact I'm a much better friend than I ever was in my married life. At this time that is all I want, friends and family to be with. I've learned to appreciate my alone time and the freedom it gives me to do what I want to do. But I still hate it when I get an attack of loneliness. Though it's less frequent as time goes by, it still leaves me feeling lost and lonely.

Donnie used to tease Nathan and Andrea about when they were going to make him a grandfather. I think Donnie realized that he had missed too much of the children's growing years and he was looking forward to enjoying the grandchildren. This Christmas they gave me a wrapped up present with a "Grammy" card inside it. So this summer I will be a Grammy and I'm looking forward to it. It will be bitter sweet because Donnie was also looking forward to it, but he won't be here to enjoy the experience with me.

Time will help me to settle down and make the right decisions for my life. Here's to support groups, to shared fears, questions, problems, and remedies with laughter and tears. Here's to camaraderie with other women, to the sisterhood. To all the good reasons for starting or joining a support group with other women who can offer so very much to help us heal. It may be the best gift you can give yourself. I often feel like a lost soul that hasn't settled down. I'm like a bouncing ball in my emotions and other widows have told me that the only thing is time.

There is nothing you or I can do about the past. It's gone and buried, but we can do a great deal about our future. We can give ourselves a chance to become all that we can be. Life is to be lived and I refuse to feel guilty that I'm alive and enjoying this life. Of course, that's easier said than done because grief still overcomes me and with it guilt and sadness. It's o.k., I let it have its time, but I make an effort to keep moving so it doesn't find a home in my soul. I have worked through numbness, anger, guilt and sadness these last two years. Not everyone goes through all these emotions, but I find comfort in knowing that I'm not alone.

I started a journal to write down the good, the bad and the ugly. It helps give me emotional release at the end of the day to put it all down on paper. Last thing at night I close my eyes and list the things I have to be thankful for. I release all my old limitations and bring peace into my life. My mind is a tool and I can choose to use it any way I wish. I work hard to think in positive affirmations, to love myself without any criticisms.

As I began to take stock of my life and make new and different choices, I perceived this stage as a period of reflection and discovery that comes of being able to look both backwards and forward with a certain measure of experience.

Feelings of distraction, distress, or emotional chaos are natural and appropriate responses to the changes going on in our lives. I saw a woman I no longer wanted to be. I had weathered the storm and it was time to heal myself. Resilience is being able to bounce back and it's critical to healing. Life's blows are so hard that it's difficult to imagine how you can rebound, but you must.

I learned that if it's a problem I can control then I need to make a specific plan and put my energy towards it. If I can't change or directly influence the problem then my only option is to move on. I took my anger and harnessed it. I used its energy to develop skills and motivate myself towards change. I would Set a Goal—Make a Plan—Do it. Commitment is vital to change. To launch the lifelong process of growing, start small, start here and start now. How much time do you have—no one knows.

I fear that my life will be over too soon and that my regrets will be for what I didn't do. When we do succeed we like to think that we did it all on our own. The truth is that success happens with a lot of faith and help from others. I believe that you can do anything with God's support and love.

It's not selfish to claim this happiness and the time it takes to arrive at the point of being "all that you can be" is your right. Watch out for the Fear of the Unknown and Fear of Failure because they will cripple your efforts to change. Live your best life by committing to something greater than yourself.

Surround yourself with positive people who will inspire and uplift you in your journey. Show a willingness to try something different. I like to try things that I've never done before. An example was taking my motorcycle driving course and getting my bike license. I haven't got a motorcycle yet, but just taking the course gave me a sense of moving forward, of doing something just for myself.

The most important thing is to know that you're here for a purpose. Starting today, you can decide to change. Change begins within you by giving of yourself to others. The only way to honor your journey is to have the courage to follow your passion. In the realm of personal change, nothing happens until you take action.

I believe that after death there will be a life review where I will have to look at my life again. I will see every missed opportunity and every failed action. Because of this I try to live with more awareness so that I won't look back and realize that I failed to do the right thing.

The best way for me to heal was to find a way to help others and stay focused on that purpose. When I'm done with this life it will be God that sees the finished product. That is the only judgment that counts. As I get older I think more about what it is all for, this life of mine.

When Donnie died I said to Holly Reid at Brenan's Funeral Home that there should be a book with a lot of different widow's stories so that a new widow can understand what's going on. Holly agreed and encouraged me to do the book.

My story is different from some because I don't have young children at home and yet I don't have the empty nest because Angela is still with me. Every widow has a different life that has been affected by her husband's death. Give yourself time to move on. Closure will come, but it has to be on your time not someone else's.

I hope that this book will remind you of the richness that is in your life. The irony is that your real wealth has nothing to do with money. Only you can make your life worthwhile, and you can do it—and so much more. You have that power if you would just believe in yourself. Starting today, you can decide to change by giving of yourself to others. You'll know when it's right because you will feel it and the courage to move forward will be there for you.

I take every opportunity to not waste my life. I think of what I want to do because I no longer have an excuse to not do it. I think, "What's your problem?" whenever I hold back from doing something I'm interested in. Usually it's fear of the unknown that holds me back.

The more you believe and move towards what you want the more people and things will come to help you get what you want. When I started the interviews I thought that I would never find enough widows that would tell me their stories with honest openness and yet God led me to them. People come into your life for a reason and they bring something to your life. Sometimes it can be a piece of humble pie, but you have to learn from it because it will make you a better person for what is still to come.

As I get older material things don't mean as much to me. What good did they do Donnie when he didn't live long enough to enjoy any of it? You play by the rules; you do everything right and then some force outside of you reaches into your life and snatches your dream right out of your hands.

Now, when you have to start your life all over, you need a support system like you've never needed one before. There's nothing as exciting as going after what you really want and getting support for it. This is no time to be a loner. You need your own buddy system to give you the courage to poke your nose into all those new doors.

You need people who are genuinely interested in how you're doing, people who will cheer you on when you do well and sympathize when things go wrong—and who will tell you to keep trying.

Don't waste your time thinking it's too late to go after your dreams. You can learn new things at any time in your life if you're willing to be a beginner, so, let's start figuring out what you want! For you to start again you'd need to be a different person with a different goal. Some things aren't replaceable. You're not going to be able to get that dream back, but you can get your life back. You can do anything you can dream of. You wouldn't dream of it if you couldn't make it happen. Your life should delight your soul with a feeling of excitement and awareness for all the opportunities you have.

The whole point of the book was that when Donnie died I had a lot of emotions and other widows are also emotional. The book shares these feelings so that we can see that it's not unusual to be emotional and unbalanced when your husband dies. It helps to talk to other widows because they understand what you're going through. This project has helped to heal me because I've learned how strong we women really are.

When I started interviewing the widows I did it for myself, for my healing. Later I thought that I should get them published, but fear told me that I couldn't do it because I didn't know anything about publishing. I had to really fight that fear by going one step at a time. I went to the library and got out books on publishing and how to do a book proposal. Then I had to build up my confidence to go for it. I just kept saying to myself that all that can happen is that they say no.

What was my excuse for not trying it? I was scared of failure and that fear almost stopped me from trying. As time went on and I gained the confidence I realized that the only thing stopping me from being the best that I can be is ME.

Everyone grieves in a different way. For me, it was important to try to make things better. To have a purpose that demanded more of me than just getting along in life. I've learned to reach out for support and in so doing I have found my purpose. I know that this book will help other widows and by doing it I have worked through my own guilt, anger and loss. Their stories are so different and yet they all have a common thread of mixed emotions.

Only another widow can share their empathy and touch your soul. It's to our credit that we care so much about each other's feelings and that we work to support and encourage each other. I like to think that you've written notes to yourself and marked passages that you felt spoke to you personally. I hope this book touches you as it has touched me.

WORDS *of* WISDOM

YOU HAVE WHAT IT TAKES TO BE

ANYTHING YOU WANT TO BE.

BE A BETTER PARENT, NEIGHBOR AND FRIEND

BY PUTTING YOURSELF OUT INTO THE WORLD.

—*Mary Francis*

Change

The winds of change came blowing across your life one day.

Little did you know the change about to come your way.

The pain you felt, the grief, the shock, no one could ever know.

But as you've read there are other wives who've had to take that blow.

They say time is a healer—you ask, can it be true?

Can the pain I feel deep in my heart, be the same for me, as you?

All who grieve will find somehow to carry on each day.

And God will give the strength you need, you simply have to pray.

—PATRICIA PERRIN

BUY A SHARE OF THE FUTURE IN YOUR COMMUNITY

These certificates make great holiday, graduation and birthday gifts that can be personalized with the recipient's name. The cost of one S.H.A.R.E. or one square foot is $54.17. The personalized certificate is suitable for framing and will state the number of shares purchased and the amount of each share, as well as the recipient's name. The home that you participate in "building" will last for many years and will continue to grow in value.

Here is a sample SHARE certificate:

YES, I WOULD LIKE TO HELP!

I support the work that Habitat for Humanity does and I want to be part of the excitement! As a donor, I will receive periodic updates on your construction activities but, more importantly, I know my gift will help a family in our community realize the dream of homeownership. **I would like to SHARE in your efforts against substandard housing in my community!** *(Please print below)*

PLEASE SEND ME _____ SHARES at $54.17 EACH = $ $_____

In Honor Of: _____

Occasion: (Circle One)   HOLIDAY   BIRTHDAY   ANNIVERSARY

　　　OTHER: _____

Address of Recipient: _____

Gift From: _____ *Donor Address:* _____

Donor Email: _____

I AM ENCLOSING A CHECK FOR $ $_____ PAYABLE TO HABITAT FOR HUMANITY OR PLEASE CHARGE MY VISA OR MASTERCARD *(CIRCLE ONE)*

Card Number _____ Expiration Date: _____

Name as it appears on Credit Card _____ Charge Amount $ _____

Signature _____

Billing Address _____

Telephone # Day _____ Eve _____

PLEASE NOTE: Your contribution is tax-deductible to the fullest extent allowed by law.
Habitat for Humanity • P.O. Box 1443 • Newport News, VA 23601 • 757-596-5553
www.HelpHabitatforHumanity.org

Printed in the USA
CPSIA information can be obtained
at www.ICGtesting.com
JSHW082203140824
68134JS00014B/396